Big Game Fishing

Hooked On Reel Fishing

Michael Clutton

Published by Michael Clutton, 2024.

BIG GAME FISHING

First edition. June 30, 2024.

Copyright © 2024 Michael Clutton.

ISBN: 979-8227667786

Written by Michael Clutton.

Table of Contents

BAIT YOUR HOOK

Welcome aboard, angling adventurers! If you've ever dreamed of wrestling a fish the size of a compact car or exchanging grumpy stares with a marlin having a bad day, you're in the right place. Explore the wild world of big game fishing with this booklet.

Why Big Game Fishing?

Why, indeed? There's an irresistible allure to big game fishing that calls to the intrepid and the mildly deranged alike. It involves more than just the act of fishing. Imagine the rush of adrenaline as you hook a bluefin tuna, the sheer force of a marlin's tug, or the thrill of a deep-sea duel with a swordfish. It's the ultimate test of patience, skill, and just a dash of lunacy.

The Humorous Importance and Appeal

Let's be honest: big game fishing isn't just a hobby. This obsession has become fully consuming. There's a reason anglers fork out thousands for high-tech gear, charter boats, and gadgets that would make James Bond jealous. It's a game where size matters, and anglers earn bragging rights through sweat, grit, and sometimes, sheer stubbornness. It's a perfect excuse to take a break, soak up the sun, and reflect on life's big questions, such as how to tell your spouse about the boat dent.

Setting the Hook

This booklet covers everything you need to know about big game fishing, including gear, techniques, hotspots, and the biggest fish. We'll give you trivia and anecdotes to impress your fishing buddies.

So, grab your gear, slather on the sunscreen, and get ready to embark on a fishing adventure like no other. Whether you're experienced or new to big game fishing, this guide has you covered with style, humor, and helpful info.

It's time to explore the depths and uncover the secrets beneath.

Chapter 1: Essential Gear and Equipment

Hook, Line, and Sinker

Bob was a man of simple pleasures—cold beer, warm sunshine, and the occasional tall tale about the one that got away. When he received his tax refund one glorious April morning, he decided it was time to invest in a serious upgrade: the latest, greatest fishing reel on the market. This engineering marvel can handle any fish effortlessly, with more features than Bob can handle.

After a few celebratory beers, Bob took his shiny new reel out for its maiden voyage. He hadn't read the manual, of course—real men don't need instructions, right? His fishing buddy, Phil, watched with a bemused grin as Bob struggled to attach the reel to his rod, a process that involved more cursing and sweating than he cared to admit.

Finally, with the reel securely in place, Bob cast his line into the sparkling blue waters. To his astonishment, he got a bite almost immediately. A big one. His rod bent close to double, and Bob's face lit up with a mix of excitement and terror. It was the moment he'd expected. The fish tugged hard, and Bob's new reel whirred to life, clicking and buzzing like an over-caffeinated cicada.

But as Bob reeled in his catch, something strange happened. The line didn't seem to get any shorter. In fact, it looked like it was getting longer. Bob's reel, in its state-of-the-art glory, had reversed itself. Instead of winding in the line, it was spooling it out at an alarming rate. The more Bob cranked, the more line spilled into the water, creating a tangled web that would have made Spider-Man proud.

By this point, Phil was doubled over with laughter. Bob, determined not to lose his prize, kept cranking, convinced he could outsmart the rebellious reel. Minutes felt like hours as the struggle continued. Bob's confidence waned, replaced by a growing realization that maybe—just maybe—he should have read the instructions.

Finally, with one last mighty effort, Bob yanked the rod back, and his line snapped with a sound like a gunshot. He fell backward into the boat, staring up at the sky, his prized reel sputtering in defeat. The fish, an unmistakable leviathan of the deep, swam off into the sunset, trailing what must have been a mile of high-end fishing line behind it.

Phil, wiping tears from his eyes, offered Bob a hand up. "Well," he said, "at least now you've got a real fishing story to tell." Bob couldn't help but laugh. He'd learned an important lesson that day: even the best gear is only as good as the fisherman using it. Glancing at instructions might have been worthwhile.

Bob's mishap with his advanced fishing reel proves that, while equipment matters, mastering its usage is even more vital. So, before you find yourself in a tangled mess like Bob, let's look at the essential equipment you'll need for big game fishing—and how to use it correctly.

Overview of Necessary Equipment

Rod and Reel: For big game fishing, you'll need a heavy-duty rod and reel capable of handling massive fish. Look for rods made from high-strength materials like graphite or fiberglass and choose reels with a high line capacity and strong drag systems.

Fishing Line: Monofilament and braided lines are popular choices for big game fishing. Monofilament offers stretch and flexibility, while braided line provides greater strength and sensitivity. The choice often depends on the specific type of fishing and preference.

Hooks: Sturdy, sharp hooks are a must. Anglers frequently use circle hooks for catch-and-release fishing because these hooks hook fish in the mouth's corner, reducing injury. J-hooks are another option but require more precise timing to set the hook correctly.

Lures and Baits: Live bait such as mackerel, squid, or bonito is highly effective in attracting big game fish. Artificial lures, including trolling lures and deep-diving plugs, can also be successful, especially when designed to mimic the appearance and movement of natural prey.

Leader: A powerful leader, usually made of wire or heavy monofilament, is essential to withstand the sharp teeth and powerful runs of big game fish. Leaders help prevent the line from being cut or abraded during the fight.

Gaffs and Nets: Once you've battled your fish up to the boat, you'll need a gaff or net to bring it aboard. Gaffs are used to hook the fish and lift it out of the water, while nets provide a safer, less injurious way to land your catch.

Fighting Belts and Harnesses: These provide support and leverage during long battles with large fish, distributing the strain across your body and reducing fatigue.

Safety Gear: Don't forget life jackets, gloves, and first-aid kits. Big game fishing can be hazardous, and it's better to be prepared for any situation.

Equipped with the right gear and a healthy respect for the instructions, you're well on your way to becoming a big game fishing legend. Just remember to laugh at the mishaps—they make the best stories.

Fresh Bait

Ancient Rods and Reels: The first fishing rods date back to ancient Egypt, around 2000 BC. Ancient Egyptians made these early rods from bamboo and used woven plant fibers to create the lines.

Medieval Hooks: In medieval Europe, people often made fish hooks from bronze. The hooks found in archaeological digs often resembled modern designs, proving that good ideas stand the test of time.

The Birth of the Reel: The fishing reel was invented in China around 1195 AD. These early reels were simple, spool-like devices attached to bamboo rods.

Shakespearean Innovation: The Shakespeare Company, founded in 1897, revolutionized fishing with the introduction of the level-wind reel, which evenly distributed line across the spool.

Fiberglass Revolution: The development of fiberglass rods in the 1940s and 1950s marked a significant improvement in rod strength and flexibility, allowing anglers to target larger species.

First Synthetic Line: Nylon fishing line, introduced in the late 1930s by DuPont, replaced traditional lines made from cotton, linen, or silk, offering greater strength and durability.

Big Game Pioneers: Big game fishing gained popularity in the early 20th century, thanks to Zane Grey and Ernest Hemingway's contributions.

Circle Hook Origins: Circle hooks, though popularized in modern times for their conservation benefits, have been used by Pacific Islander cultures for centuries, traditionally made from shell, bone, and wood.

The Role of World War II: Advances in materials technology during WWII, including the development of durable, corrosion-resistant metals, significantly improved the quality of fishing gear post-war.

Penn Reels: The Penn Fishing Tackle Manufacturing Company, founded in 1932, became famous for producing some of the most reliable and popular big game fishing reels in the world.

GPS and Sonar: The integration of GPS and sonar technology into fishing in the 1990s revolutionized the sport, allowing anglers to locate fish with unprecedented accuracy.

Braid vs. Mono: The debate between braided and monofilament lines has raged for decades. Braided lines, made from synthetic fibers like Spectra and Dyneema, offer superior strength, while monofilament lines provide stretch and abrasion resistance.

Evolution of Lures: The first artificial lures were made from wood and feathers. Modern lures use advanced materials and are designed to mimic the movements and appearance of prey fish.

First Fighting Chair: The fighting chair, an essential piece of equipment for battling big game fish, was invented in the 1930s by Michael Lerner, founder of the International Game Fish Association (IGFA).

Tag and Release: The practice of tagging and releasing big game fish for scientific study began in the 1950s, providing valuable data on fish migration, growth, and behavior.

Electrifying Reels: Electric reels, developed in the late 20th century, have made it easier to haul in deep-sea fish from great depths, reducing physical strain on anglers.

Fly Fishing for Big Game: The adaptation of fly fishing techniques for big game species like tarpon and sailfish gained popularity in the mid-20th century, requiring specialized gear and considerable skill.

Modern Composite Rods: Today's high-performance fishing rods often use composite materials, combining graphite, fiberglass, and even Kevlar to achieve the perfect balance of strength, sensitivity, and flexibility.

Game Fish Recognition: The IGFA, established in 1939, plays a crucial role in standardizing big game fishing rules and records, recognizing over 1,300 species of game fish worldwide.

Sustainable Practices: Recent innovations in gear, such as biodegradable hooks and eco-friendly lines, reflect a growing emphasis on sustainability and conservation within the fishing community.

Detailed Descriptions and Uses
Rod and Reel:

BIG GAME FISHING

Rod Description: Big game rods are typically between 5 to 7 feet long and made from durable 7materials like graphite or fiberglass. They feature a heavy action to handle the weight and power of large fish.

Reel Description: Big game reels are built to hold a significant amount of heavy line and withstand the intense drag pressure from fighting large fish. Lever drag reels are a popular choice for their precise control.

Fishing Line:

Monofilament: Made from a single strand of nylon, monofilament is versatile, easy to handle, and offers stretch to absorb shock from sudden fish movements.

Braided Line: Constructed from multiple strands of synthetic fibers, braided line is incredibly strong and thin, providing high sensitivity and minimal stretch.

Hooks:

Circle Hooks: Designed to hook fish in the corner of the mouth, reducing injury and making them ideal for catch-and-release fishing. These hooks are used for a variety of big game species.

J-Hooks: Traditional hook shape that requires precise timing to set. Often used with live bait for species like marlin and tuna.

Lures and Baits:

Live Bait: Mackerel, squid, and bonito are commonly used live baits for their natural appeal to big game fish.

Artificial Lures: Trolling lures and deep-diving plugs mimic the movement of prey, enticing big game fish to strike. These lures come in various shapes, sizes, and colors to match different target species.

Leader:

Wire Leaders: Essential when targeting toothy predators like sharks and barracuda. Made from stainless steel or titanium, these leaders prevent bite-offs.

Heavy Monofilament Leaders: Used for species with abrasive mouths, like tuna and marlin, to prevent the line from being cut during the fight.

Gaffs and Nets:

Gaffs: Long-handled hooks used to secure and lift large fish into the boat. Gaffs must be used carefully to avoid damaging the fish, especially if you plan to release it.

Nets: Large, sturdy nets provide a safer alternative for landing fish, minimizing injury and increasing the chances of successful release.

Fighting Belts and Harnesses:

Fighting Belts: Worn around the waist, these belts distribute the pressure from the rod butt, reducing fatigue during long battles.

Harnesses: Full-body harnesses provide additional support, attaching to the rod and reel to help anglers maintain leverage and control.

Safety Gear:

Life Jackets: Essential for personal safety, especially in rough seas. Modern life jackets are designed to be comfortable and non-restrictive.

Gloves: Protect hands from line cuts and provide a better grip when handling fish or gear.

First-Aid Kits: Should include supplies for treating cuts, scrapes, and other minor injuries that can occur on the water.

Frozen Bait

Rod Power: The world record for the largest fish caught on rod and reel is a great white shark weighing 2,664 pounds, captured off the coast of Australia in 1959. The sheer power required to land such a behemoth highlights the importance of using high-strength rods and reels.

Line Length: During big game fishing tournaments, it's not uncommon for anglers to spool up to 1,000 yards of line on their reels. This ensures they have enough length to handle long, powerful runs from big game fish like marlin and tuna.

Drag Force: High-end big game fishing reels can exert drag pressures exceeding 100 pounds. This immense force helps tire out large fish, making them easier to reel in, but also requires robust gear to withstand the stress.

Hook Sizes: Big game fishing hooks can range in size from a modest 5/0 (used for smaller game fish) to a hefty 20/0, which is about the size of a human hand and used for monsters like giant tuna and marlin.

Gadgetry: Some modern big game reels are equipped with digital line counters and built-in scales, allowing anglers to measure the length of the line deployed and the weight of the fish without extra equipment.

Maintenance and Care Tips

Rods and Reels:

Cleaning: After each trip, rinse your rods and reels with fresh water to remove salt and debris. Saltwater can cause corrosion, so thorough cleaning is essential.

Lubrication: Apply reel oil and grease to the appropriate parts to keep your reel functioning smoothly. Follow the manufacturer's recommendations for specific lubrication points and products.

Storage: Store rods vertically or horizontally on rod racks to prevent warping. Keep reels in a dry place, preferably covered, to protect them from dust and moisture.

Fishing Line:

Inspection: Regularly check your fishing line for signs of wear, such as fraying or nicks. Replace the line if you notice any damage, as compromised line can lead to break-offs.

Storage: Store spools of line in a cool, dark place to prevent degradation from UV light and heat. This helps maintain the line's strength and flexibility.

Hooks and Lures:

Sharpening: Keep hooks sharp using a hook file or sharpener. Sharp hooks improve your chances of a solid hookset and landing the fish.

Rust Prevention: Rinse hooks and lures with fresh water after use, and dry them thoroughly. Consider using a rust inhibitor spray for additional protection.

Leaders:

Replacement: Regularly replace leaders, especially after catching a fish. Leaders can become weakened by abrasion and bite marks, reducing their effectiveness.

Storage: Keep leaders neatly coiled and stored in a leader wallet or similar organizer to prevent tangling and damage.

Chapter 2: Fundamentals and Techniques

Hook, Line and Sinker: Tale of the Escaping Carp

In 2016, during a fishing tournament on Lake Champlain, Vermont, angler Jim McLaughlin experienced a fishing adventure that quickly became legendary among his peers. Jim, known for his patience and skill, hooked what he believed to be a sizable carp. The fish was putting up a fierce fight, and Jim was determined to reel it in.

As the battle ensued, Jim's excitement grew. The carp zigzagged through the water, testing Jim's resolve and expertise. Just as Jim began to gain the upper hand, the carp made an unexpected leap from the water, aiming directly at Jim. Startled, Jim ducked, and the carp soared over his head, landing with a splash on the other side of the boat.

The crowd of spectators on the shore burst into laughter. Jim, regaining his composure, continued to wrestle with the fish. The carp, seemingly aware of its audience, performed another aerial maneuver, this time flopping onto the boat's deck. The slippery fish wriggled furiously, sending Jim's gear flying and causing a chaotic scene.

In the midst of the pandemonium, the carp managed to slip back into the water, leaving Jim with an empty hook and a boat in disarray. The audience cheered, and Jim couldn't help but laugh at the spectacle he had inadvertently created. Despite not landing the carp, Jim's story of the "Flying Carp of Lake Champlain" became a staple at fishing gatherings, a reminder that sometimes the best catches are the ones that get away in the most unexpected ways.

Basic Techniques and Methods

Bottom Fishing: This method involves dropping bait to the bottom of the ocean and waiting for bottom-dwelling fish like grouper, snapper, and halibut to take the bait.

How to Do It:

Equipment: Use a heavy-duty rod and reel, along with a sturdy sinker to keep your bait on the bottom.

Bait: Live bait such as squid, mackerel, or cut fish is ideal.

Technique: Drop your line straight down until it hits the bottom, then reel up slightly to keep the bait just off the seabed. Wait patiently and be ready to set the hook when you feel a bite.

Trolling: Trolling involves dragging lures or bait behind a moving boat to attract predatory fish such as marlin, tuna, and wahoo.

How to Do It:

Equipment: Use a rod with a high-capacity reel and sturdy line. Trolling lures or rigged baits work best.

Speed: Maintain a steady boat speed, typically between 5 to 9 knots, depending on the target species.

Technique: Let out enough line to keep the lures or bait in the strike zone. Use outriggers to spread the lines and cover more water.

Jigging: Jigging is an active fishing technique where a lure (the jig) is rapidly moved up and down in the water to mimic the motion of a distressed fish.

How to Do It:

Equipment: Use a jigging rod and reel with a strong, braided line. Metal jigs are commonly used.

Motion: Drop the jig to the desired depth, then rapidly lift and drop the rod tip to create an enticing movement. Vary the speed and rhythm to find what works best.

Target Species: Jigging is effective for species like amberjack, tuna, and grouper.

Live Baiting: Live baiting involves using live fish as bait to attract larger predators. This technique is particularly effective for species like sailfish, kingfish, and yellowtail.

How to Do It:

Equipment: Use a sturdy rod and reel with a live bait hook and appropriate leader.

Bait: Common live baits include mackerel, herring, and pilchards.

Technique: Hook the live bait through the nose or back, allowing it to swim naturally. Free line the bait or use a small weight to keep it at the desired depth.

Surf Casting: Surf casting involves casting bait or lures from the shore into the surf zone, targeting species like striped bass, bluefish, and pompano.

How to Do It:

Equipment: Use a long surf rod and spinning reel with a heavy line.

Bait: Use live or cut bait, or artificial lures designed for surf fishing.

Technique: Cast beyond the breaking waves and let the bait settle. Keep the line tight and be ready to set the hook when you feel a bite.

Mastering these basic techniques will set you on the path to big game fishing success. Each method has its nuances and requires practice, but with patience and persistence, you'll soon find yourself reeling in impressive catches.

Fresh Bait

Ancient Egyptians and Fishing Nets: Fishing nets date back to ancient Egypt, where they were made from flax and used to catch fish in the Nile River around 3000 BC.

Chinese Innovations: The Chinese are credited with inventing fishing reels as early as the 12th century. These early reels were simple, spooling devices attached to bamboo rods.

Medieval England: During medieval times in England, fishing was not just a means of sustenance but also a regulated sport. Angling clubs and strict fishing laws were established to protect fish stocks.

Japanese Fly Fishing: Tenkara, a traditional Japanese method of fly fishing, dates back to at least the 8th century. This technique uses a simple rod, line, and fly, but no reel.

Native American Techniques: Indigenous peoples of North America used various fishing techniques, including spearfishing and weir fishing, where wooden barriers directed fish into traps.

Ice Fishing Origins: Ice fishing is believed to have originated with Native American tribes in North America, who used bone hooks and carved holes in the ice to catch fish during winter months.

Norwegian Cod Fishing: The Lofoten cod fishery in Norway is one of the oldest documented fisheries, dating back over a thousand years. This method involves longlines and is still practiced today.

Roman Fish Farming: Ancient Romans were pioneers in fish farming, creating artificial ponds to breed fish like mullet and sea bass for food and commerce.

Purse Seining: Purse seining, a method where a net encircles a school of fish and then draws tight like a purse, was developed in the 19th century and revolutionized commercial fishing.

Fly Fishing Literature: The first known book on fly fishing, "The Treatise of Fishing with an Angle," was written by Dame Juliana Berners in 1496. It remains a cornerstone of angling literature.

Spearfishing Evolution: Spearfishing, one of the oldest forms of fishing, evolved from simple wooden spears to modern spearguns and diving techniques, enabling divers to hunt fish underwater.

Trolling Development: Trolling, a technique where baited lines are drawn through the water, became popular in the early 20th century with the advent of motorized boats, allowing anglers to cover more water.

Casting Innovations: The development of spinning reels and baitcasting reels in the mid-20th century significantly improved the accuracy and distance of casts, transforming recreational fishing.

Catch-and-Release Ethic: The practice of catch-and-release fishing gained momentum in the 1950s, promoted by conservationists to ensure sustainable fish populations.

Surf Casting Evolution: Surf casting, the technique of casting bait from the shoreline into the surf, evolved with the introduction of longer rods and specialized reels, allowing anglers to reach greater distances.

Modern Jigging: Jigging, an age-old method of dropping a weighted lure and moving it up and down, became highly specialized in the late 20th century with the development of vertical jigs and sophisticated jigging rods.

Sonar Technology: The use of sonar in fishing began during WWII and became widespread in the 1950s, enabling anglers to locate fish with unprecedented accuracy.

Barbless Hooks: Barbless hooks, designed to reduce injury to fish and increase the chances of survival upon release, have been adopted by many conservation-minded anglers in recent years.

Electrofishing: Invented in the 20th century, electrofishing uses electric currents to stun fish temporarily, allowing for population studies and the collection of specimens without harm.

FADs (Fish Aggregating Devices): FADs, structures placed in open water to attract fish, have been used since ancient times and are now a crucial tool in modern commercial tuna fishing.

Advanced Strategies and Tips for Big Game Fishing

1. Kite Fishing

Description: Kite fishing involves using a kite to suspend bait on the surface of the water, creating an irresistible presentation for predatory fish.

Strategy: Position the kite so that the bait skims along the surface, mimicking the movement of an injured fish. This technique is particularly effective for sailfish and tuna.

2. Chunking

Description: Chunking involves cutting baitfish into small pieces and continuously throwing them overboard to create a chum line that attracts big game fish.

Strategy: Use a combination of large chunks for bait and smaller pieces for chum. Position your boat up-current from where you expect the fish to be, and keep a steady flow of chum going to maintain the fish's interest.

3. Deep Dropping

Description: This technique involves dropping bait to extreme depths (200 to 600 feet or more) to target species like swordfish and tilefish.

Strategy: Use electric reels or high-capacity manual reels with heavy lead weights to get your bait to the bottom quickly. Deep drop lights can also attract fish in the dark depths.

4. Live Bait Bridling

Description: Bridling involves attaching live bait to the hook in a way that allows it to swim more naturally, increasing its appeal to big game fish.

Strategy: Use a bridle rig, which typically consists of a needle and waxed floss or a rubber band. This technique keeps the hook exposed and the bait lively, making it more enticing to predators.

5. Switch and Bait

Description: This is a high-skill technique used primarily for billfish. It involves trolling teasers without hooks to attract fish, then quickly switching to a baited hook when the fish is close.

Strategy: Have a team ready with rods rigged with live or dead bait. When a fish approaches the teaser, reel in the teaser and cast the baited hook to entice a strike.

Frozen Bait

Kite Fishing Origins: Kite fishing was first developed in China over 2,000 years ago and has been adapted for modern big game fishing to target surface-feeding predators.

Swordfish Depths: Swordfish are known to dive to depths of 1,800 feet during the day, making deep dropping a challenging but rewarding technique for targeting these elusive giants.

Speed of a Sailfish: Sailfish, one of the prime targets for kite fishing, can reach speeds of up to 68 miles per hour, making them the fastest fish in the ocean.

Chumming Efficiency: A well-executed chumming strategy can increase catch rates by up to 300%, as the scent trail can draw fish from miles away to your bait.

Billfish Eyesight: Billfish have exceptional eyesight and can detect movement and color changes at great distances, making the switch and bait technique particularly effective when executed correctly.

Common Mistakes and How to Avoid Them

1. Inadequate Preparation

Mistake: Heading out to sea without proper preparation can lead to forgotten gear, insufficient bait, or mechanical failures.

How to Avoid: Create a checklist before each trip, including all necessary equipment, safety gear, and maintenance checks for your boat and tackle. This ensures you have everything you need for a successful outing.

2. Incorrect Drag Settings

Mistake: Setting the drag too tight or too loose can result in lost fish—either through broken lines or hooks pulling free.

How to Avoid: Set your drag to about one-third of your line's breaking strength. Test the drag before you start fishing to ensure it's set correctly for the species you're targeting.

3. Poor Bait Presentation

Mistake: Using poorly rigged or unnatural-looking bait can turn fish away.

How to Avoid: Take the time to rig your bait properly. Whether using live bait, dead bait, or artificial lures, make sure they look as natural as possible to entice bites.

4. Ignoring Weather and Tides

Mistake: Not considering weather conditions and tidal movements can lead to tough fishing conditions and reduced catch rates.

How to Avoid: Always check the weather forecast and tidal charts before heading out. Fish tend to be more active during certain tidal phases and in stable weather conditions.

5. Lack of Patience

Mistake: Impatience can lead to frequently changing spots or techniques, which might scare away fish or lead to missed opportunities.

How to Avoid: Practice patience and persistence. Big game fishing often requires waiting for the right moment. Trust your strategy and give it time to work before making drastic changes.

By mastering these advanced strategies and avoiding common mistakes, you'll increase your chances of success in big game fishing. Each technique requires practice and fine-tuning, but with dedication and attention to detail, you'll become a more skilled and effective angler.

Chapter 3: Types of Activities/Methods

Hook, Line and Sinker: Shark Photographer's Surprise

In 2016, Australian photographer Al McGlashan set out on what he thought would be a routine filming expedition off the coast of Port Stephens, Australia. His mission was to document the release of a tagged striped marlin, a process he had done countless times before. The marlin, a magnificent creature, had been caught and tagged by New South Wales fisheries officials and was now ready to be returned to its ocean home. McGlashan, known for his stunning underwater photography, was poised to capture this moment of freedom on film.

The day started like any other, with calm seas and clear skies providing perfect conditions for filming. McGlashan positioned himself and his equipment, ready to document the marlin's elegant swim back into the depths. The fisheries officials gently lowered the marlin into the water, and McGlashan began to film its descent.

However, as the marlin began to swim away, something unexpected and dramatic unfolded. Out of the blue, a 10-foot mako shark burst onto the scene. The shark, which had been lurking unseen, sensed an opportunity for an easy meal and charged at the marlin with lightning speed. McGlashan, caught off guard but ever the professional, kept his camera rolling, capturing every heart-pounding second.

The mako shark's attack was fierce and relentless. It circled the marlin, biting into it with powerful jaws. The water churned as the marlin struggled, but it was no match for the shark's ferocity. McGlashan's footage showed the mako tearing into the marlin, showcasing the raw power and primal instincts of these ocean predators.

For McGlashan, this was a once-in-a-lifetime shot. The footage not only captured the intensity of the shark's attack but also highlighted the unpredictable and often brutal reality of life in the ocean. What started as a simple assignment turned into a dramatic nature documentary in real-time, with McGlashan at the heart of the action.

The encounter left McGlashan and the fisheries officials in awe. They had witnessed the circle of life up close, in a way few people ever do. The footage became a sensation, drawing attention from marine biologists, conservationists, and the general public. It was a stark reminder of the ocean's untamed beauty and the fine line between predator and prey.

This story of the shark photographer's surprise is not just about the dramatic footage captured that day; it's a testament to the unpredictability of the ocean and the thrill of the unexpected. McGlashan's encounter with the mako shark transformed a routine task into an extraordinary adventure, providing a tale that would be told and retold in fishing and photography circles for years to come. It also underscored the importance of always being prepared for the unexpected, no matter how routine the task at hand may seem.

Different Approaches and Styles

When it comes to sport fishing, the variety of methods available is as vast as the ocean itself. Whether you're an old salt or a newbie angler, exploring different approaches and styles can make your fishing adventures more exciting and fruitful. Here are some popular methods, each with its unique charm and challenge.

1. Fly Fishing

Fly fishing is often seen as the poetry of angling. It involves using lightweight lures, known as flies, which mimic the insects fish feed on. This method requires a delicate touch and precise casting, making it both an art and a science.

Gear: Lightweight rods, specialized fly reels, and an assortment of flies.

Technique: The cast is everything. You'll need to master the fluid, rhythmic motion that sends the fly dancing across the water's surface.

Targets: Trout, salmon, bass, and other freshwater species, though it can be adapted for saltwater fishing as well.

2. Trolling

Trolling is the method of dragging baited lines or lures behind a moving boat. It's a fantastic way to cover a lot of water and target predatory fish that are on the hunt.

Gear: Sturdy rods, reels with a high line capacity, and trolling lures or live bait.

Technique: Maintain a consistent speed and use outriggers to spread the lines and prevent tangling.

Targets: Marlin, tuna, wahoo, and other large pelagic species.

3. Bottom Fishing

As the name suggests, bottom fishing involves dropping bait to the seabed and waiting for bottom-dwelling fish to bite. This method is straightforward and effective, especially in deep waters.

Gear: Heavy-duty rods, reels with a strong drag system, and weights to keep the bait on the bottom.

Technique: Drop your bait, wait, and prepare for a hard tug from below.

Targets: Grouper, snapper, halibut, and other species that dwell near the ocean floor.

4. Surf Casting

Surf casting is perfect for those who prefer to keep their feet on solid ground. It involves casting bait or lures from the shoreline into the surf.

Gear: Long surf rods, spinning reels, and a variety of baits and lures.

Technique: Cast beyond the breaking waves and let the bait settle. Keep the line tight and be ready for a bite.

Targets: Striped bass, bluefish, pompano, and other surf zone species.

5. Jigging

Jigging is a dynamic and active method where you repeatedly lift and drop a weighted lure to mimic the movement of distressed prey.

Gear: Jigging rods, strong braided lines, and metal jigs.

Technique: Drop the jig to the desired depth, then lift and drop the rod tip to create an enticing movement.

Targets: Amberjack, tuna, grouper, and other mid-depth to deep-sea species.

6. Spearfishing

For those who prefer a more hands-on approach, spearfishing combines snorkeling or diving with hunting fish using a speargun or pole spear.

Gear: Speargun or pole spear, diving gear, and often a wetsuit.

Technique: Dive silently, approach the fish with stealth, and aim with precision.

Targets: A wide variety, including snapper, grouper, and pelagic species.

7. Ice Fishing

Ice fishing is not for the faint of heart. This method involves fishing through a hole in the ice, usually in a frozen lake or river.

Gear: Ice auger, short sturdy rods, specialized ice fishing reels, and bait.

Technique: Drill a hole in the ice, drop your line, and wait in the chilly silence for a bite.

Targets: Walleye, perch, pike, and other cold-water species.

8. Kayak Fishing

For those who enjoy a blend of tranquility and adventure, kayak fishing allows you to reach spots inaccessible by larger boats while staying close to the water.

Gear: A stable fishing kayak, lightweight rods, and compact tackle.

Technique: Paddle quietly, position yourself strategically, and cast with precision.

Targets: Bass, redfish, trout, and other inshore species.

Benefits and Challenges of Each Type

Each fishing method offers unique benefits and presents distinct challenges. Fly fishing provides a serene, meditative experience but requires skillful casting. Trolling covers large areas and targets big game fish but demands patience and endurance. Bottom fishing is straightforward but often requires heavy gear. Surf casting keeps you grounded but demands strong casting techniques. Jigging is exciting and active but physically demanding. Spearfishing is adventurous and direct but requires diving skills and safety awareness. Ice fishing is serene yet chilly, testing your patience and resilience. Kayak fishing is peaceful and flexible but requires paddling strength and balance.

Exploring these different approaches not only broadens your fishing skills but also enriches your experience, making each trip a new adventure. So, grab your gear, choose your method, and cast away—there's a whole world of fish waiting to be discovered.

Fresh Bait

Ancient Fly Fishing: The earliest known reference to fly fishing comes from the Roman writer Claudius Aelianus in the 2nd century AD. He described Macedonian anglers using artificial flies to catch fish.

Medieval England's Fishing Law: In medieval England, fishing was heavily regulated. King Edward II even issued a decree in 1324 that all fisheries should be open to the public on Sundays.

First Fishing Rod Patent: The first patent for a fishing rod was granted in 1844 to a man named George Snyder. His invention was the precursor to the modern baitcasting reel.

Invention of Nylon Line: In the late 1930s, DuPont revolutionized fishing with the invention of nylon fishing line, replacing silk and other natural fibers which were less durable.

Trolling's Evolution: Trolling, a method now popular worldwide, was originally developed by Native Hawaiians. They used this technique to catch large fish like tuna and marlin.

Spearfishing Origins: Spearfishing is one of the oldest methods of fishing, with evidence of its practice dating back to at least 16,000 years ago. Ancient civilizations used sharpened sticks to catch fish in shallow waters.

Kayak Fishing Heritage: The Inuit people of the Arctic were the original kayak fishers. They used kayaks made from sealskin stretched over a wooden frame to hunt marine animals.

The First Fly Fishing Book: "The Treatyse of Fysshynge with an Angle" by Dame Juliana Berners, published in 1496, is considered the first known book on fly fishing.

Modern Jigging's Birth: Jigging, as we know it today, was popularized in the 1930s with the introduction of metal jigs, which provided more effective lures for deep-sea fishing.

Ice Fishing's Indigenous Roots: Native American tribes, particularly those in the Northern United States and Canada, are credited with inventing ice fishing. They used bone hooks and carved holes in the ice to catch fish during winter months.

Surf Casting Innovations: Surf casting gained popularity in the 19th century. Anglers in coastal towns developed longer rods and heavier lines to cast bait farther into the surf.

Kite Fishing's Ancient Beginnings: Kite fishing, first developed in China over 2,000 years ago, was adapted by Polynesians who used kites to position baited lines beyond the breakers.

Tuna Fishing Pioneers: Big-game tuna fishing took off in the early 20th century, with pioneers like Zane Grey and Ernest Hemingway bringing attention to the sport through their adventurous exploits and writings.

Electrofishing: Invented in the 20th century, electrofishing uses electric currents to temporarily stun fish, allowing scientists to study fish populations without harming them.

GPS in Fishing: The introduction of GPS technology in the 1990s transformed fishing, allowing anglers to pinpoint the best fishing spots with unprecedented accuracy.

Tag and Release: Tag and release programs started in the 1950s have significantly contributed to our understanding of fish migration patterns and population dynamics.

Barbless Hooks for Conservation: In recent years, barbless hooks have become popular in catch-and-release fishing for their ability to reduce injury to fish and increase survival rates upon release.

First Fishing Competitions: Organized fishing competitions date back to the 19th century, with the first recorded fishing tournament held in New York in 1864.

Surfboard Fishing: In the 1960s, surfers in California began using their boards to paddle out to deeper waters for fishing, giving rise to a niche method known as surfboard fishing.

Women in Fly Fishing: Women have been a part of fly fishing history for centuries. Dame Juliana Berners, mentioned earlier, and Joan Wulff, a champion fly caster in the mid-20th century, have both made significant contributions to the sport.

Benefits and Challenges of Each Type

Fly Fishing

Benefits:

Highly rewarding and meditative.

Excellent for catching trout and other freshwater species.

Promotes environmental awareness and conservation.

Challenges:

Steep learning curve for casting techniques.

Requires patience and precision.

Can be gear-intensive and expensive.

Trolling

Benefits:

Covers large areas and targets big game fish.

Great for deep-sea fishing and offshore expeditions.

Allows for a relaxed fishing experience from a boat.

Challenges:

Can be boring during slow periods.

Requires a boat and often specialized gear.

Fuel and boat maintenance can be costly.

Bottom Fishing

Benefits:

Effective for catching a variety of bottom-dwelling species.

Simple technique suitable for all skill levels.

Often yields larger fish.

Challenges:

Requires heavy-duty gear.

Can be physically demanding.

Risks of snagging on the seabed.

Surf Casting

Benefits:

Allows fishing from the shore.

Targets a variety of surf zone species.

Offers a dynamic and engaging fishing experience.

Challenges:

Requires strong casting skills and technique.

Dependent on weather and surf conditions.

Gear can be cumbersome to transport.

Jigging

Benefits:

Highly active and engaging.

Effective for deep-sea and mid-water species.

Can be done from boats or the shore.

Challenges:

Physically demanding.

Requires specialized jigs and rods.

Fish may not always respond to jigging motion.

Spearfishing

Benefits:

Direct and hands-on approach.

Sustainable and selective method.

Combines diving and fishing for an adventurous experience.

Challenges:

Requires diving skills and safety knowledge.

Limited to clear water and good visibility.

Physically demanding and potentially dangerous.

Ice Fishing

Benefits:

Provides a unique and serene fishing experience.

Effective for winter fishing.

Can be a social activity with ice shanties and groups.

Challenges:

Requires special equipment and clothing.

Dependent on weather and ice conditions.

Patience is essential due to slower action.

Kayak Fishing

Benefits:

Offers access to hard-to-reach spots.

Provides a peaceful and close-to-nature experience.

Promotes physical fitness and paddling skills.

Challenges:

Limited storage and space for gear.

Requires good paddling and balance.

Can be challenging in rough water or strong currents.

Each fishing method comes with its own set of benefits and challenges, but the diversity of approaches ensures that there's something for every angler's preference and skill level. Whether you seek the tranquility of fly fishing or the thrill of spearfishing, the world of sport fishing offers endless opportunities for adventure and discovery.

Frozen Bait

Record-Setting Trolling: The world record for the largest marlin caught by trolling was set in 1953 by Alfred Glassell Jr., who landed a black marlin weighing 1,560 pounds off the coast of Peru.

Ancient Spearfishing Techniques: Spearfishing can be traced back to prehistoric times, with evidence of harpoons found in caves in Southern France dating back over 16,000 years.

Kayak Fishing Popularity: Kayak fishing has seen a massive rise in popularity in recent years. According to the Outdoor Foundation's 2021 report, nearly 4.5 million people in the U.S. participated in kayak fishing, a significant increase from previous years.

Fly Fishing Records: The largest fish caught on a fly rod is a 385-pound lemon shark, caught by Tom Evans in 1982 in the Florida Keys. This remarkable feat demonstrates the versatility and potential of fly fishing even in big game scenarios.

Ice Fishing Expeditions: The largest ice fishing tournament in the world is the Brainerd Jaycees Ice Fishing Extravaganza in Minnesota. Held annually on Gull Lake, it attracts over 10,000 participants each year, braving sub-zero temperatures for a chance at prizes and glory.

Choosing the Right Method for You

Selecting the right fishing method depends on several factors, including your experience level, target species, location, and personal preferences. Here's a guide to help you decide which method might be best suited for your next fishing adventure.

Consider Your Experience Level

Beginner: If you're new to fishing, consider starting with methods that have a gentle learning curve, such as **bottom fishing** or **surf casting**. These methods are straightforward and allow you to focus on the basics of handling gear and understanding fish behavior.

Intermediate: For those with some experience, **trolling** and **kayak fishing** offer opportunities to hone your skills. These methods involve more technique and strategic planning, providing a good challenge without being overly complex.

Advanced: Seasoned anglers might enjoy the technical challenges of **fly fishing**, **jigging**, or **spearfishing**. These methods require precision, practice, and a deeper understanding of fish habits and environments.

Identify Your Target Species

Freshwater Species: If you're aiming to catch trout, bass, or salmon, **fly fishing** and **bottom fishing** in rivers and lakes are ideal choices. These methods are tailored to the behavior of freshwater fish.

Saltwater Species: For larger saltwater targets like marlin, tuna, or sailfish, **trolling** and **jigging** are highly effective. These methods are designed to cover large areas and attract predatory fish.

Both: Some methods, such as **kayak fishing** and **surf casting**, are versatile enough to be used in both freshwater and saltwater environments, depending on the species present in the area.

Evaluate Your Location

Shore-Based: If you prefer fishing from the shore, **surf casting** and **fly fishing** in streams are excellent options. They allow you to access productive fishing spots without needing a boat.

Boat-Based: For those with access to a boat, **trolling** and **bottom fishing** in deeper waters can be incredibly rewarding. Boats provide mobility and the ability to reach otherwise inaccessible fishing grounds.

Specialized Environments: Ice fishing is perfect for winter enthusiasts who want to experience fishing in frozen lakes. Similarly, **spearfishing** is ideal for clear, warm waters where diving is feasible.

Match Your Personal Preferences

Adventure and Physical Activity: If you enjoy a hands-on, active approach, **kayak fishing** and **spearfishing** offer the excitement of physical engagement and direct interaction with your environment.

Relaxation and Patience: For a more relaxed experience, methods like **bottom fishing** or **trolling** allow you to sit back and wait for the fish to come to you, providing ample time to enjoy the scenery and serenity of the water.

Technical Mastery: If you take pleasure in mastering intricate techniques, **fly fishing** and **jigging** offer a rewarding challenge with their emphasis on skillful casting and precise lure action.

Sorting Out the Keepers

Choosing the right fishing method is all about aligning your interests, skills, and fishing goals. Whether you're seeking the peaceful solitude of fly fishing or the adrenaline rush of spearfishing, there's a method out there that's perfect for you. Consider what you enjoy most about fishing, and let that guide your decision. Happy fishing!

Chapter 4: Popular Locations and Hotspots

Hook, Line and Sinker: Tale of the Kayak Angler and the Relentless Barracuda

In 2012, Florida Sportsman member Palm Beach Pete set out for what he thought would be a routine day of kayak fishing in the Bermuda Triangle. Pete, an experienced angler, was no stranger to the quirks of kayak fishing, but nothing could have prepared him for the day's adventure.

Pete launched his kayak on a clear morning, the sun casting a golden glow over the calm waters. His target was the elusive and fast-moving barracuda, a fish known for its fierce fight and impressive speed. Armed with his trusty rod and a cooler full of bait, Pete paddled out with high hopes.

Things started to go awry when Pete realized he had forgotten to secure his bait cooler. As he reached back to grab it, the cooler tipped, sending bait fish flopping into the kayak and the water. Amid the chaos, Pete noticed a large shadow beneath the surface—a barracuda, drawn by the commotion.

Eager to salvage the situation, Pete cast his line. The barracuda struck almost immediately, its razor-sharp teeth snapping at the bait. The force of the strike nearly pulled Pete from his kayak. The battle was on, with the barracuda darting under the kayak, circling with lightning speed, and leaping out of the water in a show of strength.

Just as Pete thought he had the upper hand, the barracuda made a final, desperate lunge. It hit the side of the kayak, knocking Pete's paddle into the water. Now drifting and at the mercy of the relentless fish, Pete clung to his rod with one hand while trying to retrieve his paddle with the other.

To add to the spectacle, another angler nearby had witnessed the commotion and paddled over to help. The sight of two men in kayaks, one wrestling with a formidable barracuda and the other trying to assist, drew laughter and cheers from onlookers on the shore.

Finally, with a combined effort, Pete and his fellow angler managed to subdue the barracuda. Exhausted but triumphant, Pete hoisted the fish into his kayak, where it flopped and thrashed, adding a few more nicks and scrapes to the already battle-worn vessel.

Back on shore, Pete's tale of the relentless barracuda became an instant hit. The story was retold at fishing clubs and gatherings, a humorous reminder of the unpredictability of the ocean and the thrill of the unexpected. Pete's kayak, scarred from the encounter, stood as a testament to the wild adventure, while the barracuda's fierce fight became a legend among local anglers.

This real-life fishing escapade not only highlights the challenges and excitement of kayak fishing in the Bermuda Triangle but also underscores the camaraderie and humor that often accompany such adventures.

Top Locations for Sport Fishing

Cairns, Australia

Target Species: Black Marlin, Sailfish, Tuna

Highlights: The Great Barrier Reef is not only a natural wonder but also a hotspot for some of the largest marlins in the world. Cairns is often dubbed the "Black Marlin Capital of the World."

Key West, Florida, USA

Target Species: Sailfish, Tarpon, Bonefish

Highlights: Known for its rich variety of species and excellent year-round fishing conditions, Key West offers both deep-sea and flats fishing. The annual Hemingway International Billfish Tournament is a major draw.

Cabo San Lucas, Mexico

Target Species: Striped Marlin, Dorado, Roosterfish

Highlights: Cabo is renowned for its impressive marlin fishing, often with several caught in a single day. The iconic Arch of Cabo San Lucas provides a stunning backdrop.

Prince Edward Island, Canada

Target Species: Bluefin Tuna

Highlights: This location offers some of the best bluefin tuna fishing in the world, with giants often weighing over 1,000 pounds. The picturesque scenery is an added bonus.

Phuket, Thailand

Target Species: Sailfish, Marlin, Giant Trevally

Highlights: Phuket's warm waters are teeming with exotic fish. The annual Phuket International Sportsfishing Tournament attracts anglers from around the globe.

Bermuda

Target Species: Wahoo, Yellowfin Tuna, Blue Marlin

Highlights: Bermuda's waters are known for their clarity and abundance of big game fish. The island hosts several prestigious fishing tournaments, including the Bermuda Triple Crown.

Hatteras, North Carolina, USA

Target Species: Bluefin Tuna, Yellowfin Tuna, Mahi Mahi

Highlights: Known as the "Blue Marlin Capital of the World," Hatteras offers some of the best offshore fishing on the East Coast. The warm Gulf Stream waters attract a variety of species.

Martha's Vineyard, Massachusetts, USA

Target Species: Striped Bass, Bluefish, Bonito

Highlights: This iconic island is famous for the Martha's Vineyard Striped Bass and Bluefish Derby, one of the oldest and most storied fishing tournaments in the U.S.

Malindi, Kenya

Target Species: Sailfish, Marlin, Broadbill

Highlights: The Kenyan coast offers some of the best sport fishing in Africa, with the Pemba Channel being particularly renowned for its variety and size of catches.

New Zealand

Target Species: Kingfish, Snapper, Marlin

Highlights: The waters around New Zealand are famed for their diverse and plentiful fish populations. The Bay of Islands and the Three Kings Islands are especially popular with anglers.

Each of these locations offers unique fishing experiences, diverse marine life, and breathtaking natural beauty, making them top choices for sport fishing enthusiasts worldwide.

Fresh Bait

Birthplace of Sport Fishing: The concept of sport fishing as we know it today began in the 15th century in England with the publication of "The Treatyse of Fysshynge with an Angle" by Dame Juliana Berners, which is considered one of the first known books on the subject.

Hemingway's Favorite Spot: Ernest Hemingway, a passionate angler, spent much of his time fishing in the waters off Key West and Cuba. His boat, Pilar, is legendary in the sport fishing world.

The First Marlin Record: The first officially recorded marlin catch was by Zane Grey, an American author and big game fisherman, who caught a 1,036-pound marlin in Tahiti in 1930.

Cairns' Marlin Boom: In the 1960s, Cairns, Australia, became famous for its marlin fishing when giant black marlins were discovered in the Great Barrier Reef area, drawing anglers from around the world.

Martha's Vineyard Derby: The Martha's Vineyard Striped Bass and Bluefish Derby, established in 1946, is one of the oldest and most prestigious fishing tournaments in the United States.

Bermuda's First Fishing Tournament: Bermuda's first international fishing tournament was held in 1954, attracting anglers from across the globe and helping to establish the island as a premier sport fishing destination.

Prince Edward Island's Giants: In the 1970s, Prince Edward Island gained fame for its giant bluefin tuna, with many fish weighing over 1,000 pounds, making it a top destination for big game fishing.

Phuket's Fishing Evolution: Sport fishing in Phuket, Thailand, has grown significantly since the 1980s, transforming the region into a hotspot for catching sailfish and marlin, thanks to the abundant marine life and favorable fishing conditions.

Hatteras' Gulf Stream Advantage: Hatteras, North Carolina, benefits from the nearby Gulf Stream, which brings warm water and a variety of fish species close to shore, making it a prime location for sport fishing.

Kenya's Pemba Channel: The Pemba Channel off the coast of Kenya has been a renowned sport fishing destination since the 1950s, known for its rich marine biodiversity and record-breaking catches of marlin and sailfish.

New Zealand's Three Kings Islands: The Three Kings Islands of New Zealand are legendary for their kingfish and snapper fishing, attracting anglers from around the world since the mid-20th century.

Cabo San Lucas' Bisbee's Black & Blue Tournament: Cabo San Lucas hosts Bisbee's Black & Blue Marlin Tournament, one of the richest sport fishing tournaments globally, with millions of dollars in prizes.

Bermuda Triangle Mystique: Despite its reputation for mysterious disappearances, the Bermuda Triangle is also known for its rich fishing grounds, particularly for wahoo and tuna.

Hemingway's International Billfish Tournament: Established in 1950, the Hemingway International Billfish Tournament in Cuba is one of the oldest and most prestigious sport fishing competitions in the Caribbean.

Zane Grey's Angling Club: Zane Grey, the famous author, founded the Tuna Club of Avalon in 1898 in Catalina Island, California, which is one of the oldest and most prestigious sport fishing clubs in the world.

Norwegian Cod Wars: The Lofoten Islands in Norway have been a significant fishing area for centuries, and the "Cod Wars" of the 1950s and 1970s were a series of confrontations over fishing rights between the UK and Iceland.

The Rise of Ice Fishing: Ice fishing gained popularity in North America in the 19th century, with Native American techniques evolving into modern ice fishing practices.

Surf Casting Origins: Surf casting as a popular sport began in the 19th century along the coasts of Europe and the United States, with specialized equipment and techniques developing over time.

First Offshore Oil Rig Tournament: In 1947, the first sport fishing tournament held on an offshore oil rig took place in the Gulf of Mexico, highlighting the unique fishing opportunities these structures provide.

The Role of WWII: Advances in materials technology during WWII, such as the development of fiberglass, significantly improved the quality of fishing rods and reels, revolutionizing sport fishing equipment.

Seasonal and Regional Variations

Sport fishing is heavily influenced by seasonal and regional variations, which affect fish behavior, migration patterns, and availability. Understanding these variations is crucial for successful fishing trips.

Seasonal Variations

Spring:

Freshwater: Many freshwater species, such as bass and trout, become more active as the water warms. This is a prime time for fly fishing and bait casting in lakes and rivers.

Saltwater: In coastal areas, spring brings an increase in fish activity as species like striped bass and bluefish begin their migrations to spawn.

Summer:

Freshwater: Warm water temperatures lead to increased feeding activity in fish like pike and carp. Early mornings and late evenings are the best times to fish.

Saltwater: Offshore fishing peaks for species like marlin, tuna, and sailfish. Warm, calm waters are ideal for trolling and deep-sea fishing.

Fall:

Freshwater: Fish prepare for winter by feeding aggressively. Salmon and trout fishing is excellent as these species spawn in rivers and streams.

Saltwater: Coastal waters see an influx of species like redfish, snook, and flounder. Cooler temperatures often lead to increased fish activity, making it a prime season for inshore fishing. Many species, such as striped bass, also migrate during the fall, offering excellent fishing opportunities along their routes.

Winter:

Freshwater: Ice fishing becomes the primary method in northern regions. Species like walleye, perch, and pike are popular targets beneath the frozen surfaces of lakes and rivers.

Saltwater: In warmer climates, winter fishing can be productive for species like grouper, snapper, and kingfish. Anglers often head to tropical destinations to escape the cold and continue their fishing pursuits. Additionally, some areas, such as the Florida Keys, offer peak fishing seasons for sailfish and other game fish during the winter months.

Regional Variations

North America:

East Coast: Known for striped bass, bluefish, and tuna. Seasonal migrations heavily influence fishing strategies.

West Coast: Offers excellent opportunities for salmon, halibut, and various offshore species like tuna and marlin. The cooler Pacific waters and strong currents contribute to a rich marine ecosystem.

Gulf Coast: Famous for redfish, snapper, and tarpon. The warm, shallow waters provide ideal conditions for inshore fishing throughout much of the year.

Caribbean:

Top Species: Sailfish, marlin, and tarpon. The warm, clear waters make it a year-round destination for sport fishing.

Seasonal Peaks: Winter and spring are the best times for billfish, while summer is excellent for tarpon.

Australia:

Great Barrier Reef: Famous for black marlin, especially from September to December. The reef's biodiversity offers year-round fishing opportunities.

Southern Waters: Known for tuna and shark fishing, with summer months being the most productive.

Africa:

East Coast (Kenya): The Pemba Channel is renowned for marlin and sailfish, with the best season from November to March.

West Coast (South Africa): Offers excellent tuna and yellowtail fishing, particularly during the summer months (December to February).

Europe:

Mediterranean: Offers diverse fishing opportunities for species like bluefin tuna and swordfish. Summer and fall are the peak seasons.

Northern Waters: The North Sea and Norwegian fjords are famous for cod and halibut, with winter being a prime time for fishing under the northern lights.

Asia:

Southeast Asia (Phuket, Thailand): Known for sailfish and marlin, with year-round fishing due to the tropical climate.

Japan: Offers unique fishing experiences for species like yellowtail and tuna, with peak seasons varying by region.

Understanding the seasonal and regional variations in sport fishing can help anglers plan more effective trips, targeting specific species at their most active times and locations. This knowledge not only increases the chances of a successful catch but also enhances the overall fishing experience.

Frozen Bait

Cairns' Marlin: Cairns, Australia, is known for having some of the largest black marlins, with specimens often exceeding 1,000 pounds.

Hatteras' Gulf Stream: The Gulf Stream near Hatteras, North Carolina, brings a variety of fish close to shore, creating one of the most diverse fishing environments in the US.

Bermuda's Wahoo Run: Bermuda's waters are famous for their annual wahoo run, which peaks in the fall and attracts anglers worldwide.

Phuket's Sailfish: Phuket, Thailand, is one of the few places where anglers can catch sailfish year-round.

New Zealand's Kingfish: The waters around New Zealand's Three Kings Islands are known for producing some of the largest yellowtail kingfish in the world.

Local Tips and Tricks

Cairns, Australia:
Best Time to Fish: September to December for black marlin.
Local Tip: Use large live baits like tuna or mackerel to attract giant marlins.
Key West, Florida, USA:
Best Time to Fish: April to June for tarpon.
Local Tip: Fish around bridges and channels during outgoing tides for the best tarpon action.
Cabo San Lucas, Mexico:
Best Time to Fish: October to November for marlin.
Local Tip: Trolling with brightly colored lures works well for marlin and dorado.
Prince Edward Island, Canada:
Best Time to Fish: July to October for bluefin tuna.
Local Tip: Charter a local guide who knows the best tuna spots and techniques.
Phuket, Thailand:
Best Time to Fish: November to March for sailfish.
Local Tip: Use kite fishing techniques to present baits naturally on the surface.
Bermuda:
Best Time to Fish: May to September for blue marlin.
Local Tip: Fish the offshore banks and seamounts where marlin are known to congregate.
Hatteras, North Carolina, USA:
Best Time to Fish: May to September for tuna.
Local Tip: Use ballyhoo rigged with a sea witch for trolling to attract tuna and other pelagic species.
Martha's Vineyard, Massachusetts, USA:
Best Time to Fish: September to October for striped bass.
Local Tip: Fish at night during the new moon for the biggest stripers.
Malindi, Kenya:
Best Time to Fish: December to March for marlin and sailfish.
Local Tip: Troll with natural baits like ballyhoo and mullet for best results.
New Zealand:
Best Time to Fish: January to April for kingfish.

Local Tip: Jigging around offshore pinnacles and reefs is highly effective for kingfish.

Chapter 5: Targeting Specific Fish Species

Hook, Line and Sinker: Tale of the Misguided Marlin

In 2015, during the Big Rock Blue Marlin Tournament in North Carolina, a team of anglers aboard the aptly named "Out of Control" had an encounter that became the talk of the fishing world. Captain Bill and his crew had spent hours trolling the deep waters without a bite. Just as spirits began to wane, the line snapped taut with a force that nearly yanked the rod from its holder. "It's a big one!" Captain Bill shouted, and the battle commenced.

The marlin on the other end was no ordinary fish. It leaped spectacularly from the water, displaying its impressive size and agility, much to the awe of the crew. However, this marlin had a peculiar knack for complicating things. Instead of a straightforward fight, it zigzagged erratically, circled the boat, and even dove under it multiple times. The crew struggled to keep up, with lines tangling and chaos ensuing.

At one point, the marlin performed an acrobatic leap right over the boat, leaving the crew ducking and scrambling to avoid its sharp bill. This unexpected maneuver was followed by a splash so enormous that it drenched everyone on board. Laughter erupted, albeit nervously, as the realization hit them: this marlin was out to make fools of them.

The battle continued for nearly two hours, each side gaining and losing ground. The marlin seemed to toy with the anglers, diving deep and then shooting back up with bewildering speed. Captain Bill, with decades of experience, admitted later that he'd never encountered such a spirited fish.

Finally, with a combination of skill and sheer determination, the crew managed to bring the marlin alongside the boat. Its size was breathtaking, an estimated 800 pounds of pure muscle. As they prepared to haul it in, the marlin gave one last defiant twist, snapping the leader line and vanishing into the deep with a final flick of its tail.

Exhausted and soaked, the crew stared at the empty space where their prize had been. Captain Bill broke the silence with a hearty laugh. "Well, boys, that's a story for the ages!" And indeed, it was. The tale of the Misguided Marlin quickly spread, becoming a favorite recounting among anglers at the marina and beyond.

This story not only highlighted the unpredictability of big game fishing but also underscored the respect and admiration that such a formidable opponent commands. Sometimes, the best stories aren't about the fish you catch but the ones that get away, leaving behind memories—and a lot of laughter.

Profiles of Key Targets

1. Largemouth Bass

Description: One of the most popular freshwater game fish, known for its aggressive nature and thrilling fight.

Habitat: Found in lakes, rivers, and ponds across North America.

Techniques: Effective methods include topwater lures, plastic worms, and crankbaits. Early mornings and late afternoons are prime times.

2. Bluefin Tuna

Description: A highly prized saltwater game fish, renowned for its size and strength.

Habitat: Found in the Atlantic and Pacific Oceans, often in deep, offshore waters.

Techniques: Trolling with live bait or lures, and using heavy tackle to handle their powerful runs.

3. Rainbow Trout

Description: A beautiful and popular freshwater fish, known for its vibrant colors and acrobatic fights.

Habitat: Found in cold, clear streams, rivers, and lakes in North America and other parts of the world.

Techniques: Fly fishing with dry flies or nymphs, and using spinners or small crankbaits.

4. Sailfish

Description: Recognized by its distinctive sail-like dorsal fin, this fast and acrobatic saltwater fish is a favorite among sport fishers.

Habitat: Found in warm ocean waters around the world, particularly in the Atlantic and Pacific Oceans.

Techniques: Kite fishing, trolling with ballyhoo, and live baiting near surface structures.

5. Northern Pike

Description: Known for its elongated body and sharp teeth, the pike is a fierce predator and exciting catch.

Habitat: Found in freshwater lakes and rivers across the Northern Hemisphere.

Techniques: Using large spinners, spoons, and live baitfish. Targeting weed beds and submerged structures is effective.

Fresh Bait

Oldest Fish: The coelacanth was thought to be extinct for 65 million years until a live specimen was found in 1938. This "living fossil" dates back to the time of the dinosaurs.

Ancient Lineage: Sturgeon, often called "living relics," have existed for more than 200 million years, surviving through various extinction events.

Fastest Fish: The sailfish is the fastest fish in the ocean, capable of swimming at speeds up to 68 miles per hour.

Longest Lifespan: The orange roughy can live for over 150 years, making it one of the longest-living fish.

Best Practices for Each Target

Largemouth Bass

Techniques:

Topwater Lures: Effective during early morning and late evening when bass are feeding on the surface.

Plastic Worms: Use Texas or Carolina rigs in weedy areas to avoid snags.

Crankbaits: Ideal for covering large areas quickly and triggering reaction strikes.

Habitat: Found in lakes, rivers, and ponds with ample cover such as weed beds, submerged structures, and fallen trees.

Bluefin Tuna

Techniques:

Trolling: Use live bait or lures designed to mimic the prey of tuna. Heavy tackle is necessary to handle their powerful runs.

Chumming: Helps to attract tuna to the boat. Once they are in the vicinity, switch to live bait for the best chance of a hookup.

Jigging: Effective when tuna are feeding deep. Use heavy jigs and strong lines.

Habitat: Prefers deep offshore waters in the Atlantic and Pacific Oceans, often found near underwater structures like seamounts and drop-offs.

Rainbow Trout

Techniques:

Fly Fishing: Use dry flies, nymphs, and streamers depending on the trout's feeding habits. Match the hatch to the local insect population.

Spinners and Small Crankbaits: Effective in fast-moving streams and rivers. Brightly colored lures often yield the best results.

Bait Fishing: Use worms, salmon eggs, or artificial baits. Float fishing or bottom fishing methods work well.

Habitat: Found in cold, clear streams, rivers, and lakes. They thrive in oxygen-rich waters with temperatures between 50-60°F.

Sailfish

Techniques:

Kite Fishing: Keeps bait on the water's surface, creating an irresistible presentation for sailfish.

Trolling: Use ballyhoo or other small fish. Combine with colorful skirts to add attraction.

Live Baiting: Drift live bait near surface structures where sailfish are known to hunt.

Habitat: Warm ocean waters worldwide, particularly in the Atlantic and Pacific Oceans. They are often found near the surface, especially around reefs and drop-offs.

Northern Pike

Techniques:

Large Spinners and Spoons: Use bright, flashy lures to provoke aggressive strikes. Retrieve at varying speeds to trigger a response.

Live Baitfish: Hook live bait such as minnows or perch on a quick-strike rig for best results.

Jerkbaits: Effective in shallow waters, especially in spring and fall when pike are more active.

Habitat: Freshwater lakes and rivers across the Northern Hemisphere. They prefer areas with dense vegetation and submerged structures where they can ambush prey.

Frozen Bait

Marlin Speed Records: The black marlin holds the record for the fastest recorded fish, reaching speeds of up to 82 miles per hour (132 km/h).

Longest Recorded Fish Migration: The European eel undertakes one of the longest migrations of any fish species, traveling over 3,700 miles (6,000 kilometers) from European rivers to the Sargasso Sea to spawn.

Depth Divers: The Cuvier's beaked whale, while not a fish, holds the record for the deepest dive among marine animals, reaching depths of 9,874 feet (3,008 meters). This record is often mistakenly attributed to fish, highlighting the incredible capabilities of marine life .

Endurance Swimmers: Atlantic bluefin tuna can swim across the entire Atlantic Ocean from North America to Europe and back in a single year, demonstrating their incredible endurance and navigational abilities .

Record Catfish: The largest recorded catfish was a Mekong giant catfish caught in Thailand in 2005, weighing an astounding 646 pounds (293 kilograms) .

Case Studies and Success Stories

Case Study: The Restoration of Salmon in the Columbia River

The Columbia River, once home to some of the largest salmon runs in the world, saw a drastic decline in salmon populations due to overfishing, habitat loss, and dam construction. In response, comprehensive restoration efforts were undertaken involving multiple stakeholders, including government agencies, Native American tribes, and environmental organizations.

Success Factors:

Habitat Restoration: Efforts focused on restoring spawning and rearing habitats, including removing barriers to fish migration and improving water quality.

Dam Management: Implementing fish ladders and other modifications at dams to facilitate salmon migration.

Hatchery Programs: Supplementing wild populations with hatchery-raised fish while ensuring genetic diversity.

Regulatory Measures: Implementing fishing regulations to prevent overharvesting and protect critical life stages of salmon.

Results:

Significant increases in salmon populations have been observed, with some runs returning to levels not seen in decades. The successful restoration project has resulted in:

Enhanced Biodiversity: Improved conditions have allowed for the resurgence of other aquatic species dependent on healthy salmon populations.

Economic Benefits: The revival of the salmon runs has revitalized local economies, boosting commercial and recreational fishing industries.

Cultural Impact: Native American tribes, whose traditions and livelihoods are closely tied to salmon, have seen a restoration of cultural practices and improved food security.

Sustainable Practices: The project has set a precedent for sustainable fishery management, influencing policies and practices in other regions .

Case Study: The Comeback of the Striped Bass in the Chesapeake Bay

The striped bass population rebounded significantly, leading to the lifting of the fishing moratorium. This success story includes:

Sustainable Fishery: Striped bass is now sustainably managed, with regulations ensuring the long-term health of the population.

Economic Growth: The recovery has supported local economies, providing jobs and income through recreational fishing and tourism.

Environmental Awareness: The project raised awareness about the importance of pollution control and habitat conservation, fostering greater community involvement in environmental stewardship.

Scientific Advancements: Research and monitoring efforts have led to better understanding and management of fish populations, benefiting other conservation initiatives .

Success Story: The Revival of Lake Victoria's Nile Perch Fishery

The Nile perch population has shown signs of recovery, and the fishery is on a path to sustainability. Key outcomes include:

Improved Food Security: The recovery of the Nile perch has helped improve food security for communities around Lake Victoria. The increased fish populations provide a reliable source of protein and nutrition for local people .

Economic Stability: Sustainable management practices have stabilized the fishery, ensuring long-term economic benefits for local fishers. This has included better enforcement of fishing regulations, which has reduced illegal fishing and allowed fish stocks to recover.

Environmental Improvements: Efforts to control invasive species, such as the water hyacinth, and improve water quality have enhanced the overall health of the lake's ecosystem. This has not only benefited the Nile perch but also other native species that depend on a healthy aquatic environment .

Regional Collaboration: The success underscores the importance of cooperation among neighboring countries (Kenya, Uganda, and Tanzania) in managing shared natural resources. Joint management initiatives have included coordinated enforcement and shared research efforts .

Chapter 6: Advanced Topics and Technology

Hook, Line, and Sinker: The Smart Fish and the Overconfident Angler

In 2019, a group of marine biologists off the coast of New Zealand made headlines with an extraordinary encounter that combined advanced technology with an unexpected twist. Dr. Emily Thompson and her team were testing a new underwater drone designed to track and study large fish in their natural habitat. The drone, equipped with high-definition cameras and sophisticated sonar, promised to revolutionize marine research.

The team chose a notorious local haunt known for its population of massive yellowtail kingfish, a prized catch among anglers. The drone, nicknamed "Deep Blue," was deployed into the clear waters, its cameras streaming live footage back to the research vessel.

Everything was going smoothly until a particularly curious kingfish, dubbed "Moby" by the team for its impressive size, decided to investigate the new intruder in its territory. Moby, a seasoned fish known to local fishermen for its elusiveness, circled the drone with a mix of caution and curiosity.

Dr. Thompson, watching the live feed, joked, "Looks like Moby wants to be the next marine biologist." The team laughed, but what happened next left them all stunned. Moby began to interact with the drone in a way no one expected. The fish nudged the drone gently at first, then with increasing force, as if testing its resilience.

Suddenly, the drone's sonar picked up a school of smaller fish nearby, and Moby's behavior changed. It started to herd the school towards the drone, using it as a makeshift barrier. The team watched in amazement as the kingfish demonstrated a level of intelligence and strategy that was unprecedented.

"Moby's using the drone to fish!" Dr. Thompson exclaimed. The kingfish had effectively turned the advanced piece of technology into a tool for its own hunting. It was a remarkable display of adaptability and intelligence, something rarely documented in wild fish.

The spectacle didn't end there. As Moby successfully corralled and captured several fish, it seemed to regard the drone with what could only be described as satisfaction before swimming off into the depths. The team, still processing what they had witnessed, realized they had just observed a significant moment in marine biology.

The incident highlighted not only the remarkable capabilities of marine life but also the unexpected consequences of introducing advanced technology into natural habitats. The story of Moby and the underwater drone quickly spread, becoming a favorite tale among marine biologists and anglers alike.

This anecdote serves as a humorous reminder that no matter how advanced our technology gets, nature always finds a way to surprise us. Sometimes, the fish are smarter than we think!

Advancements in Fishing Gear

Smart Reels: These modern fishing reels are equipped with digital displays that show line length, depth, and water temperature. Advanced models can connect to smartphones, enabling anglers to track and share their catches in real-time.

Electric Reels: Ideal for deep-sea fishing, these reels have built-in motors to assist in hauling heavy catches from great depths, reducing physical strain and making it easier to reel in large fish like swordfish and tuna.

High-Resolution Fish Finders: Utilizing advanced sonar technology, these devices provide detailed underwater images, distinguishing between different fish species and structures, thereby making targeting specific species easier.

Biodegradable Fishing Line: To address environmental concerns, manufacturers have developed fishing lines that naturally break down over time, reducing the impact on marine ecosystems while maintaining strength and durability during use.

LED Lures: These innovative lures emit light to mimic bioluminescent prey, making them especially effective for night fishing and targeting species attracted to light, such as squid and certain predatory fish.

Technological Innovations

Drone Fishing: Drones are being used to deploy bait to precise locations that are otherwise hard to reach. Equipped with cameras, they provide a bird's-eye view of potential fishing spots, allowing anglers to scout for fish schools from above.

GPS-Enabled Trolling Motors: These motors allow for precise boat control and positioning. With GPS integration, anglers can set waypoints, follow depth contours, and maintain a steady position over a school of fish without manual adjustments.

Wearable Tech: Smartwatches and other wearable devices can now track weather patterns, tides, and moon phases, all of which influence fish behavior. These devices can also sync with fish finders and other fishing gear to provide a comprehensive overview of the fishing environment.

Underwater Cameras: Portable underwater cameras provide real-time video feeds of the underwater environment, allowing anglers to see how fish react to their bait and adjust their techniques accordingly. Some models also record footage for later review.

Environmental and Conservation Efforts

Artificial Reefs: Designed to promote marine life, these structures provide habitats for fish and other marine organisms. Made from environmentally friendly materials, artificial reefs can help restore fish populations and support biodiversity.

Catch and Release Improvements: Innovations such as barbless hooks and fish-friendly nets are designed to minimize harm to fish during capture, supporting conservation efforts by increasing the survival rates of released fish.

Sustainable Bait: Researchers are developing synthetic baits that mimic the texture and scent of live bait. These alternatives reduce the need for harvesting live bait, which can deplete local ecosystems.

Future Trends

Artificial Intelligence (AI): AI is being integrated into fish finders and other fishing equipment to analyze patterns and predict where fish are likely to be. This technology can help anglers make more informed decisions and increase their success rates.

Biodegradable Gear: Continued development in biodegradable fishing gear aims to reduce environmental impact, with innovations like water-soluble hooks and eco-friendly lines.

Virtual Reality (VR) Fishing Simulators: These are becoming popular for training and entertainment. VR simulators provide realistic fishing experiences, allowing anglers to practice techniques and strategies in a controlled environment.

Underwater Drones: Future underwater drones equipped with cameras and sensors could provide live feeds and detailed underwater maps, helping anglers to spot fish and understand underwater terrain better than ever before.

Smart Rods: Advanced fishing rods with built-in sensors could measure cast distance, hook tension, and fish behavior, relaying data to smartphones to help improve technique and success rates.

In summary, while technology continues to enhance the fishing experience, it's important to remember that nothing replaces the thrill of the chase, the patience required, and the joy of being out on the water. Whether using a bamboo stick or a high-tech rod, the essence of fishing remains the same—a blend of skill, patience, and a bit of luck.

Fresh Bait

Ancient Fly Fishing: The earliest known reference to fly fishing comes from the Roman writer Claudius Aelianus in the 2nd century AD. He described Macedonian anglers using artificial flies to catch fish.

Medieval Fishing Laws: In medieval England, fishing was heavily regulated. King Edward II issued a decree in 1324 that all fisheries should be open to the public on Sundays .

First Fishing Rod Patent: The first patent for a fishing rod was granted in 1844 to a man named George Snyder. His invention was the precursor to the modern baitcasting reel .

Invention of Nylon Line: In the late 1930s, DuPont revolutionized fishing with the invention of nylon fishing line, replacing silk and other natural fibers .

Trolling's Evolution: Trolling, now popular worldwide, was originally developed by Native Hawaiians to catch large fish like tuna and marlin .

Spearfishing Origins: Spearfishing is one of the oldest methods of fishing, with evidence of its practice dating back to at least 16,000 years ago. Ancient civilizations used sharpened sticks to catch fish in shallow waters .

Kayak Fishing Heritage: The Inuit people of the Arctic were the original kayak fishers. They used kayaks made from sealskin stretched over a wooden frame to hunt marine animals .

The First Fly Fishing Book: "The Treatyse of Fysshynge with an Angle" by Dame Juliana Berners, published in 1496, is considered the first known book on fly fishing .

Modern Jigging's Birth: Jigging, as we know it today, was popularized in the 1930s with the introduction of metal jigs which provided more effective lures for deep-sea fishing.

Ice Fishing's Indigenous Roots: Native American tribes, particularly those in the Northern United States and Canada, are credited with inventing ice fishing. They used bone hooks and carved holes in the ice to catch fish during winter months.

Surf Casting Innovations: Surf casting gained popularity in the 19th century. Anglers in coastal towns developed longer rods and heavier lines to cast bait farther into the surf.

Kite Fishing's Ancient Beginnings: Kite fishing first developed in China over 2000 years ago and was adapted by Polynesians who used kites to position baited lines beyond the breakers.

Tuna Fishing Pioneers: Big-game tuna fishing took off in the early 20th century with pioneers like Zane Grey and Ernest Hemingway bringing attention to the sport through their adventurous exploits and writings.

Electrofishing: Invented in the 20th century, electrofishing uses electric currents to temporarily stun fish, allowing scientists to study fish populations without harming them.

GPS in Fishing: The introduction of GPS technology in the 1990s transformed fishing, allowing anglers to pinpoint the best fishing spots with unprecedented accuracy.

Tag and Release: Tag and release programs started in the 1950s have significantly contributed to our understanding of fish migration patterns and population dynamics.

Barbless Hooks for Conservation: In recent years, barbless hooks have become popular in catch-and-release fishing for their ability to reduce injury to fish and increase survival rates upon release.

First Fishing Competitions: Organized fishing competitions date back to the 19th century, with the first recorded fishing tournament held in New York in 1864.

Surfboard Fishing: In the 1960s, surfers in California began using their boards to paddle out to deeper waters for fishing, giving rise to a niche method known as surfboard fishing.

Women in Fly Fishing: Women have been a part of fly fishing history for centuries. Dame Juliana Berners and Joan Wulff, a champion fly caster in the mid-20th century, have both made significant contributions to the sport .

High-Tech Gear and Gadgets

Smart Reels: These modern fishing reels come equipped with digital displays that show line length, depth, and water temperature. Some advanced models can connect to smartphones, allowing anglers to track their catches and share them on social media in real-time.

Electric Reels: Particularly useful for deep-sea fishing, these reels have built-in motors to help haul in heavy catches from great depths, reducing physical strain on the angler and making it easier to reel in large fish like swordfish and tuna .

High-Resolution Fish Finders: Using advanced sonar technology, these devices provide detailed images of the underwater environment. They can distinguish between different types of fish and underwater structures, making it easier for anglers to target specific species .

Biodegradable Fishing Line: To address environmental concerns, manufacturers have developed fishing lines that break down naturally over time, reducing the impact on marine ecosystems. These lines are designed to be strong and durable during use but will decompose if lost in the water .

- **LED Lures**: These lures emit light, mimicking the bioluminescence of prey in deep and murky waters. They are especially effective for night fishing and targeting species that are attracted to light, such as squid and certain types of predatory fish.

- **Drone Fishing**: Drones are being used to deliver bait to precise locations that are otherwise hard to reach. Equipped with cameras, these drones can also scout for fish schools from above, giving anglers a bird's-eye view of potential fishing spots.

- **GPS-Enabled Trolling Motors**: These motors allow for precise boat control and positioning. With GPS integration, anglers can set waypoints, follow depth contours, and maintain a steady position over a school of fish without manual adjustments.

- **Wearable Tech**: Smartwatches and other wearable devices can now track weather patterns, tides, and moon phases, all of which influence fish behavior.

These devices can also sync with fish finders and other fishing gear to provide a comprehensive overview of the fishing environment.

- **Underwater Cameras**: Portable underwater cameras provide real-time video feeds of the underwater environment. Anglers can use these to see how fish are reacting to their bait and adjust their techniques accordingly. Some models also record footage for later review.

- **Artificial Reefs**: Designed to promote marine life, these structures provide habitats for fish and other marine organisms. Made from environmentally friendly materials, artificial reefs can help restore fish populations and support biodiversity.

- **Catch and Release Improvements**: Innovations such as barbless hooks and fish-friendly nets are designed to minimize harm to fish during capture. This supports conservation efforts by increasing the survival rates of released fish.

- **Sustainable Bait**: Researchers are developing synthetic baits that mimic the texture and scent of live bait. These alternatives reduce the need for harvesting live bait, which can deplete local ecosystems.

- **AI in Fish Finders**: Artificial intelligence is being integrated into fish finders and other fishing equipment to analyze patterns and predict where fish are likely to be. This technology can help anglers make more informed decisions and increase their success rates.

- **VR Fishing Simulators**: These are becoming popular for training and entertainment. VR simulators provide realistic fishing experiences, allowing anglers to practice techniques and strategies in a controlled environment.

- **Eco-Friendly Gear**: As environmental awareness grows, there is an increasing demand for eco-friendly fishing gear. This includes everything from biodegradable hooks to solar-powered boats, aiming to reduce the ecological footprint of fishing activities.

- **Smart Rods**: Advanced fishing rods with built-in sensors could measure cast distance, hook tension, and fish behavior, relaying data to smartphones to help improve technique and success rates.

- **Future Underwater Drones**: Future underwater drones equipped with cameras and sensors could provide live feeds and detailed underwater maps, helping anglers to spot fish and understand underwater terrain better than ever before.

Frozen Bait

Deep Sea Discoveries: Modern fish finders and underwater drones have led to the discovery of previously unknown marine species and underwater structures, significantly expanding our understanding of marine ecosystems.

Record-Setting Technology: The world record for the deepest recorded fish catch using an electric reel was set at a depth of over 6,000 feet. This showcases the incredible advancements in fishing technology allowing anglers to reach extreme depths.

LED Lures Success: Studies have shown that LED lures can increase catch rates by up to 30% in deep-sea fishing, as the light attracts fish that are otherwise difficult to lure in dark, murky waters.

AI in Angling: Artificial intelligence in fish finders can analyze water conditions, fish behavior, and historical data to predict the best fishing spots, improving catch rates by an estimated 20%.

Biodegradable Lines: The introduction of biodegradable fishing lines has reduced the impact of lost lines in marine environments, with these lines decomposing within five years compared to traditional lines that can take up to 600 years.

Future Trends

Smart Fishing Gear: The future of fishing gear includes rods and reels embedded with sensors that provide real-time feedback on fish activity, water conditions, and even angler performance. These "smart" tools will help anglers improve their techniques and increase their success rates.

Advanced AI Systems: Future fish finders will be powered by even more advanced AI systems capable of learning from each fishing trip. These systems will offer personalized advice, predicting the best times and locations to fish based on past experiences and real-time data.

Eco-Friendly Innovations: The fishing industry will continue to focus on sustainability with the development of fully biodegradable hooks, nets, and other gear. This innovation aims to minimize the ecological footprint of fishing activities, ensuring the preservation of marine habitats.

Virtual Reality Training: VR fishing simulators will become more sophisticated, offering realistic training experiences that mimic various fishing conditions and environments. This technology will allow anglers to practice and refine their skills without ever leaving home.

Underwater Robotics: The use of underwater drones and robots will become more prevalent, aiding in everything from scouting fishing spots to tagging and studying marine life. These advancements will provide anglers with unprecedented insights into underwater ecosystems and fish behavior.

Chapter 7: Safety and Best Practices

Hook, Line, and Sinker: The Overloaded Boat

In 2016, a group of friends from Texas decided to take their annual fishing trip to a nearby lake. The group, known for their love of fishing and barbecues, rented a small pontoon boat for the weekend. The boat, designed for a maximum of eight passengers, ended up carrying twelve eager fishermen along with coolers, fishing gear, and an impressive array of barbecue equipment.

As they set out onto the lake, spirits were high. The grill was fired up, and the beers were flowing. The extra weight on the boat caused it to sit lower in the water, but nobody seemed to mind. The friends joked about how they were "living large" on their floating paradise.

However, trouble began when one of the friends, Jim, noticed that the boat was taking on water. "Hey guys, I think we're sinking!" he shouted, more amused than alarmed. His friends laughed it off, attributing his concern to the few beers he'd already had.

But Jim was right. The boat, overloaded and unbalanced, was indeed sinking. Water started pouring in faster, and the friends quickly realized the gravity of the situation. Panic ensued as they scrambled to grab life jackets and abandon their barbecue feast. Coolers and fishing gear were tossed overboard in a desperate attempt to lighten the load.

In the chaos, the boat capsized, sending everyone into the water. Fortunately, they were not far from shore, and all managed to swim to safety. The sight of twelve grown men clinging to floating coolers and barbecue grills, while their prized pontoon boat sank, was a spectacle that drew laughter from onlookers on the shore.

The local fire department arrived to rescue the sodden group and tow the wrecked boat back to the dock. The friends, soaked and sheepish, had learned a valuable lesson about boating safety and the importance of adhering to weight limits.

This story, widely shared among the local fishing community, serves as a humorous reminder that safety should always come first, even when you're having a great time. Jim, who had initially raised the alarm, earned the nickname "Captain Safety," and the group never overloaded a boat again.

Safety Guidelines and Precautions

Always Wear a Life Jacket: Regardless of your swimming ability, always wear a life jacket when on a boat. Ensure it fits properly and is in good condition.

Check Weather Conditions: Always check the weather forecast before heading out. Avoid fishing during storms or high winds, and be prepared for sudden changes.

Boat Capacity: Adhere to the boat's weight limit and passenger capacity. Overloading can lead to capsizing or sinking.

Safety Equipment: Ensure your boat is equipped with essential safety gear, including life jackets, flares, a fire extinguisher, a first-aid kit, and a whistle.

Stay Hydrated and Sun-Protected: Bring plenty of water and protect yourself from the sun with sunscreen, a hat, and sunglasses. Heat exhaustion and sunburn can be serious issues during long days on the water.

File a Float Plan: Let someone know your fishing plans, including where you're going and when you expect to return. This can be crucial in case of an emergency.

Avoid Alcohol: Save the drinks for after your fishing trip. Alcohol impairs judgment and coordination, increasing the risk of accidents.

Know Your Limits: Don't push yourself beyond your physical limits. If you're tired or unwell, take a break. Fishing should be enjoyable, not exhausting.

Proper Handling of Fish and Gear: Use tools like pliers and gloves to handle fish safely, avoiding injury to yourself and the fish. Dispose of hooks and fishing line properly to prevent accidents and environmental harm.

Be Aware of Local Regulations: Follow local fishing regulations, including size and bag limits, to ensure sustainable fishing practices.

Emergency Procedures: Familiarize yourself with basic first aid and emergency procedures. Know how to respond to common fishing-related injuries, such as cuts or hooks in the skin.

Night Fishing Precautions: If you plan to fish at night, ensure your boat has proper lighting and carry a flashlight or headlamp. Stay aware of your surroundings and maintain communication with your group.

Fresh Bait

First Life Jackets: The earliest form of life jacket, known as the "Cork Waistcoat," was invented by Captain John Ross Ward in 1854. Made from blocks of cork sewn into a vest, it was designed to keep shipwrecked sailors afloat.

Coast Guard Formation: The U.S. Coast Guard was established in 1790 as the Revenue Marine. Its primary mission was to enforce tariffs and combat smuggling, but it has since evolved into a multifaceted organization dedicated to maritime safety, security, and environmental stewardship.

Emergency Beacons: The Emergency Position Indicating Radio Beacon (EPIRB) was introduced in the 1970s. These devices have saved countless lives by sending distress signals to satellites, which then relay the information to search and rescue teams.

Flare Guns: First used in the early 20th century, flare guns have been a critical part of maritime safety, providing a visual signal to rescuers during emergencies. The bright, colorful flares can be seen from miles away, even in daylight.

VHF Radios: Very High Frequency (VHF) radios became standard equipment for boats in the 1950s. They allow for direct communication with the Coast Guard and other vessels, ensuring rapid response in case of emergencies.

Hypothermia Awareness: The awareness of hypothermia and its dangers became prominent in the 20th century, leading to better safety protocols for cold-water fishing and boating. Proper clothing and emergency procedures have saved many lives.

Personal Locator Beacons (PLBs): Introduced in the 1990s, PLBs are compact, handheld devices that send distress signals to satellites. They have become an essential safety tool for solo anglers and remote expeditions.

First Aid Kits: Comprehensive first aid kits became widely available in the mid-20th century, offering essential supplies to treat injuries on the water, from minor cuts to more severe wounds.

Fire Extinguishers: The requirement for fire extinguishers on boats became standard in the mid-1900s, significantly improving safety by allowing boaters to quickly address onboard fires.

Navigation Lights: Mandated by maritime law, navigation lights became essential for preventing collisions at night or in poor visibility. Different colored lights indicate the type and direction of the vessel.

Float Plans: The practice of filing a float plan—informing someone onshore about your trip details—gained popularity in the late 20th century. It ensures that rescuers have vital information if you don't return on time.

Carbon Monoxide Detectors: Awareness of carbon monoxide poisoning led to the installation of detectors on boats in the late 20th century, preventing accidents from engine exhaust fumes.

Man Overboard Systems: These systems, which alert the crew if someone falls overboard, have been developed with advanced technology to automatically detect and respond to such incidents.

Self-Inflating Life Jackets: These modern life jackets automatically inflate upon contact with water, providing immediate buoyancy and reducing the risk of drowning.

Marine Safety Courses: The proliferation of marine safety courses, often required for boat licenses, has significantly increased boater education and safety awareness.

Improved Distress Signals: The development of high-intensity strobe lights and other advanced distress signals has improved visibility and response times during rescues.

Fire Suppression Systems: Automatic fire suppression systems, installed in engine compartments, can detect and extinguish fires quickly, preventing catastrophic damage.

Waterproof Gear: Advances in waterproof gear, including clothing and bags, ensure that essential items like communication devices and first aid supplies remain dry and functional.

Kill Switch Lanyards: These safety devices, which shut off the engine if the operator falls overboard, became standard equipment in the late 20th century, preventing runaway boats.

Enhanced Weather Forecasting: Advances in meteorology and technology provide boaters with accurate weather forecasts, helping them avoid hazardous conditions.

Ethical Considerations

Sustainability: Adhering to sustainable fishing practices is crucial. Overfishing not only depletes fish populations but also disrupts marine ecosystems. Anglers should follow regulations regarding catch limits and target species that are not endangered.

Catch and Release: When practicing catch and release, it's important to handle fish gently to minimize stress and injury. Use barbless hooks, wet your hands before handling fish, and release them quickly back into the water to ensure their survival.

Waste Management: Proper disposal of waste, including fishing lines, hooks, and bait packaging, is essential to prevent pollution and protect wildlife. Anglers should always carry a trash bag and dispose of waste responsibly.

Respecting Marine Life: Avoid disturbing marine habitats and wildlife. Anchoring on coral reefs, for instance, can cause significant damage. Use designated anchoring spots and be mindful of the environment.

Fishing Ethics: Respect other anglers and their space. Avoid crowding fishing spots and follow local etiquette to ensure a pleasant experience for everyone. Additionally, always seek permission before fishing on private property.

Supporting Conservation: Participate in and support conservation efforts. Many organizations work to protect fish habitats and promote sustainable fishing practices. Donations, volunteer work, and spreading awareness can make a significant impact.

By following these ethical guidelines, anglers can help preserve the environment and ensure that fishing remains a sustainable and enjoyable activity for future generations.

Frozen Bait

Drowning Statistics: According to the World Health Organization, drowning is the third leading cause of unintentional injury death worldwide, with an estimated 236,000 deaths annually. A significant portion of these drownings occur during recreational activities, including fishing.

Life Jacket Effectiveness: Studies show that wearing a life jacket can reduce the risk of drowning by 50%. Despite this, a 2017 report revealed that about 80% of boating deaths involved drowning, and 83% of those victims were not wearing life jackets.

Boating Accidents: The U.S. Coast Guard reported 4,168 boating accidents in 2019, resulting in 613 deaths and 2,559 injuries. Operator inattention, improper lookout, operator inexperience, excessive speed, and alcohol use were the top five primary contributing factors.

Emergency Beacon Success: Since their introduction, Emergency Position Indicating Radio Beacons (EPIRBs) have significantly improved search and rescue operations. According to NOAA, EPIRBs have helped save over 43,000 lives worldwide since 1982.

Hypothermia Risk: Water temperatures as high as 70°F (21°C) can lead to hypothermia. Cold water rapidly robs the body of heat, and hypothermia can set in within minutes, severely impairing motor skills and mental capacity.

Environmental Impact

Pollution Reduction: Modern biodegradable fishing lines and hooks are designed to minimize environmental impact. Traditional fishing lines can take up to 600 years to decompose, causing significant harm to marine life. Biodegradable alternatives break down within five years, reducing this threat.

Wildlife Protection: Lost fishing gear, also known as "ghost gear," poses a severe risk to marine wildlife. It is estimated that ghost gear accounts for 10% of ocean plastic pollution and can trap and kill marine animals for decades.

Habitat Preservation: Sustainable fishing practices, such as catch and release, help preserve fish populations and habitats. Proper handling techniques and the use of barbless hooks ensure that released fish have a higher survival rate, maintaining the ecological balance.

Ecosystem Impact: Overfishing and unsustainable practices can lead to the depletion of key species, disrupting the entire marine ecosystem. Anglers adhering to regulations and quotas help protect species from extinction and ensure healthy fish populations.

Artificial Reefs: The creation of artificial reefs using environmentally safe materials provides new habitats for marine life. These structures enhance biodiversity and offer new opportunities for recreational fishing, while also relieving pressure on natural reefs.

By understanding the environmental impacts of fishing activities and adopting responsible practices, anglers can contribute to the conservation of marine ecosystems and ensure the sustainability of the sport for future generations.

Chapter 8: A Tackle Box Full of Sport Fishing Trivia

Welcome to the treasure trove of tantalizing tidbits! This chapter is packed with eyebrow-raising trivia from the world of big game fishing. Get ready to impress your fishing buddies with these fascinating facts.

Fastest Fish: The sailfish can swim at speeds up to 68 miles per hour, making it the fastest fish in the ocean.

Oldest Fish: The coelacanth, once thought extinct, was rediscovered in 1938. This "living fossil" dates back to the time of the dinosaurs.

Deepest Divers: Swordfish can dive to depths of 1,800 feet during the day.

Largest Marlin: The largest marlin ever caught on rod and reel was a black marlin weighing 1,560 pounds, caught by Alfred Glassell Jr. off the coast of Peru in 1953.

Marlin Speed Records: The black marlin holds the record for the fastest recorded fish, reaching speeds of up to 82 miles per hour.

Longest Migration: The European eel undertakes one of the longest migrations of any fish species, traveling over 3,700 miles from European rivers to the Sargasso Sea to spawn.

Fishing Reels' Origin: Fishing reels were invented in China around 1195 AD.

Ancient Fishing Rods: The first fishing rods date back to ancient Egypt around 2000 BC, made from bamboo.

Longest Swordfish Fight: The longest recorded swordfish fight lasted 32 hours, fought by angler Louis Marron off the coast of Chile in 1953.

Shakespearean Innovation: The Shakespeare Company revolutionized fishing with the introduction of the level-wind reel in 1897.

Fiberglass Revolution: The development of fiberglass rods in the 1940s and 1950s marked a significant improvement in rod strength and flexibility.

Largest Freshwater Fish: The largest freshwater fish ever caught was a giant freshwater stingray, weighing approximately 660 pounds, caught in the Mekong River in Cambodia in 2022.

Oldest Fishing Hook: The oldest known fishing hooks were made from sea snail shells and are estimated to be 23,000 years old, discovered in a cave on Okinawa Island, Japan.

Largest Tarpon: The largest tarpon ever caught weighed 286 pounds, and was landed in 2003 off the coast of Guinea-Bissau, West Africa.

Oldest Fishery: The Lofoten cod fishery in Norway is over a thousand years old.

First Fish Finder: The first commercial fish finder, the Furuno FAX-1, was developed in Japan in 1948, revolutionizing how anglers locate fish underwater.

irst Fishing License: The first fishing license was issued in the United States in 1902 in the state of Oregon, to regulate and conserve fish populations.

Most Expensive Fishing Rod: The Oyster Bamboo Fly Rod, handcrafted by Bill Oyster, is one of the most expensive fishing rods in the world, with prices reaching up to $10,000.

Longest Fish: The oarfish, known as the "king of herrings," holds the record for the longest bony fish. It can grow up to 36 feet in length, and sightings of this elusive deep-sea giant often inspire tales of sea serpents.

Smart Reels: Modern reels feature digital line counters and built-in scales.

Longest Fishing Rod: The longest fishing rod ever built was 22.45 meters (about 73.6 feet) long, constructed by fishing enthusiasts in Japan and recognized by the Guinness World Records in 2019.

Largest Swordfish: The largest swordfish ever caught weighed 1,182 pounds and was landed off the coast of Chile in 1953 by Louis Marron.

Record Marlin Catch: Zane Grey caught a 1,036-pound marlin in Tahiti in 1930, the first officially recorded marlin catch.

Longest Fishing Expedition: The longest continuous fishing expedition lasted for 56 days, set by a commercial fishing vessel in the North Pacific in 2015. This record highlights the endurance and challenges faced by deep-sea fishermen.

Ice Fishing Origins: Native American tribes in North America pioneered ice fishing.

Trolling's Hawaiian Roots: Native Hawaiians developed trolling to catch large fish like tuna and marlin.

Japanese Fly Fishing: Tenkara, a traditional Japanese fly fishing method, dates back to at least the 8th century.

BIG GAME FISHING

Strangest Catch - In 2015, a fisherman in Florida caught a prosthetic leg while fishing in the Gulf of Mexico? The leg was returned to its owner, who had lost it while swimming at a nearby beach. This unusual catch is a reminder that you never know what might be lurking beneath the waves!

Electric Reels - High-end electric reels, which assist anglers in hauling in heavy catches from great depths, can exert drag pressures exceeding 100 pounds. This immense force helps tire out large fish, making them easier to reel in but also requires robust gear to withstand the stress.

Giant Bluefin Tuna - The largest bluefin tuna ever caught weighed a staggering 1,496 pounds. This colossal fish was reeled in off the coast of Nova Scotia in 1979 and remains a testament to the incredible size and power of these ocean giants.

Electric Eels - Electric eels generate electric shocks of up to 600 volts. While not typically a target for sport fishing, these powerful fish are fascinating and highlight the diverse capabilities of aquatic creatures.

World Record Catfish - The largest recorded catfish was a Mekong giant catfish caught in Thailand in 2005, weighing an astounding 646 pounds. This massive catch showcases the incredible size that some freshwater fish can reach.

Swordfish Depths - Swordfish are known to dive to depths of 1,800 feet during the day, making deep-dropping a challenging but rewarding technique for targeting these elusive giants.

Women in Fly Fishing: Dame Juliana Berners and Joan Wulff have made significant contributions to the sport.

Tarpon Leaps - Tarpons are known for their spectacular leaps out of the water when hooked. These aerial acrobatics can be as high as 10 feet, providing an exhilarating challenge for anglers trying to reel them in.

GPS in Fishing: Introduced in the 1990s, GPS technology transformed fishing by pinpointing the best spots.

Piranha Myths - Piranhas have a fearsome reputation, but most species are actually timid and scavengers. Only a few species have been known to attack large animals, and these incidents are rare and usually involve provoked or stressed fish.

Tag and Release: Began in the 1950s, providing valuable data on fish migration and behavior.

Underwater Drones: Equipped with cameras and sensors, these drones help spot fish and understand underwater terrain.

Deep-Sea Fish Light - Many deep-sea fish, such as the lanternfish, possess bioluminescent organs that emit light. This ability helps them navigate the dark depths, attract prey, and communicate with each other in their pitch-black environment.

Biodegradable Gear: Innovations like water-soluble hooks and eco-friendly lines aim to reduce environmental impact.

First Fishing Rod Patent: Granted in 1844 to George Snyder, this invention was the precursor to the modern baitcasting reel.

Electrofishing: Invented in the 20th century, electrofishing uses electric currents to study fish populations.

Kite Fishing: Developed over 2,000 years ago in China and adapted by Polynesians.

Catch-and-Release Practices - Catch-and-release fishing, promoted to conserve fish populations, involves handling fish minimally and using barbless hooks to increase their survival rate after being released back into the water.

Chumming Efficiency: A well-executed chumming strategy can increase catch rates by up to 300%.

Fly Fishing's First Literature: "The Treatyse of Fysshynge with an Angle" remains a cornerstone of angling literature.

Mola Mola Sunfish - The ocean sunfish, or mola mola, is the heaviest bony fish in the world, with some individuals weighing over 2,000 pounds. These gentle giants are often seen basking on the ocean surface, which helps them regulate their body temperature.

FADs: Fish Aggregating Devices have been used since ancient times and are crucial in modern commercial fishing.

Hemingway's International Billfish Tournament: Established in 1950, this is one of the oldest and most prestigious fishing competitions in the Caribbean.

Epilogue

As we cast our lines and reel in the last chapters of this angling adventure, let's reflect on the exhilarating journey we've embarked upon together. From the primordial rivers of ancient Egypt to the cutting-edge technology of today's high-tech fishing gear, we've delved into the depths of sport fishing's rich history and diverse practices. We've learned about the evolution of fishing techniques, marveled at the innovative minds behind revolutionary equipment, and chuckled at the humorous and often unexpected tales from the fishing frontlines.

Sport fishing isn't just a hobby; it's a blend of art, science, patience, and a bit of luck. It's about the thrill of the chase, the joy of the catch, and the stories that become legendary over time. Whether you're a seasoned angler or a curious novice, the world of sport fishing offers endless opportunities to test your skills, explore new waters, and connect with nature in profound and meaningful ways.

We've covered everything from the basics of essential gear and fundamental techniques to advanced strategies and targeting specific fish species. Along the way, we've sprinkled in fascinating trivia and historical tidbits to enhance your appreciation of this timeless pursuit. Each chapter aimed to equip you with knowledge, inspire you with stories, and entertain you with the quirks and curiosities of the fishing world.

Further Exploration

As we wrap up this booklet, consider it just the beginning of your fishing expedition. The waters are vast, and there are countless fish waiting to challenge and delight you. Take what you've learned here and apply it to your next fishing trip. Experiment with different techniques, explore new fishing spots, and continue to educate yourself about the diverse species that inhabit our oceans, rivers, and lakes.

Remember, the best anglers never stop learning. Stay curious, ask questions, and seek advice from fellow fishing enthusiasts. Join fishing clubs, participate in local tournaments, and share your experiences and knowledge with others. The camaraderie and shared passion within the fishing community are invaluable resources that can enrich your journey.

Lastly, always practice sustainable and ethical fishing. Respect the environment, follow local regulations, and contribute to conservation efforts to ensure that future generations can enjoy the same thrills and wonders that sport fishing provides today.

So, grab your gear, head to your favorite fishing spot, and cast your line into the unknown. Who knows what incredible stories and unforgettable experiences await you beneath the surface? Tight lines and happy fishing!

References

The Complete Book of Fishing Knots, Leaders, and Lines by Lindsey Philpott
A comprehensive guide to essential fishing knots and rigging techniques.
A History of Fishing by Richard Schweid
An in-depth look at the cultural and technological evolution of fishing through the ages.
The Old Man and the Sea by Ernest Hemingway
A classic novel that captures the spirit and struggle of big game fishing.
Fishing for Dummies by Peter Kaminsky
An accessible and informative guide for beginners and experienced anglers alike.
Zane Grey: Outdoorsman by Thomas H. Pauly
A biography of the legendary author and angler, highlighting his contributions to sport fishing.
The Complete Angler by Izaak Walton
A timeless piece of literature that explores the joys and philosophies of fishing.
Modern Fish Act - National Oceanic and Atmospheric Administration (NOAA)
Information on current fishing regulations and conservation efforts.
International Game Fish Association (IGFA) World Record Game Fishes - Annual publication
The definitive guide to world record catches and sport fishing achievements.
The Fisherman's Ocean by David A. Ross
An insightful guide to understanding oceanography and its effects on fishing.
Bluewater Gold Rush by Tom Kendrick
The true story of divers in the California sea cucumber fishery, offering a unique perspective on underwater harvesting.
Tales of the Angler's Eldorado: New Zealand by Zane Grey
Adventures and exploits of Zane Grey in one of the world's premier fishing destinations.

Fishing Through the Apocalypse by Matthew L. Miller

A modern take on fishing and conservation, exploring the future of angling in a changing world.

Recommended Reading

The Hungry Ocean by Linda Greenlaw

A memoir by one of the world's only female swordfishing captains, detailing the challenges and adventures of commercial fishing.

Cod: A Biography of the Fish that Changed the World by Mark Kurlansky

A fascinating historical account of the cod fishery and its impact on global economies and cultures.

In the Heart of the Sea: The Tragedy of the Whaleship Essex by Nathaniel Philbrick

The true story that inspired Moby-Dick, highlighting the perils of 19th-century whaling.

The Longest Silence: A Life in Fishing by Thomas McGuane

A collection of essays reflecting on the author's lifelong passion for fishing.

Fly Fishing Through the Midlife Crisis by Howell Raines

A personal journey and memoir that intertwines fly fishing with the author's experiences and reflections on life.

Don't miss out!

Visit the website below and you can sign up to receive emails whenever Michael Clutton publishes a new book. There's no charge and no obligation.

https://books2read.com/r/B-A-IAFJB-JBKPD

BOOKS 2 READ

Connecting independent readers to independent writers.

Did you love *Big Game Fishing*? Then you should read *Bloodlines: The Juice Chronicles*[1] by Michael Clutton!

[2]

If a single dad can survive financial woes, dual love interests, an annoying mother, and a growing list of gory murders—staying alive long enough to save the world should be easy, right?

Dak, a struggling entrepreneur, stumbles onto an impossible product he dubs 'Juice,' slamming him into a heart-pounding fast-forward effort to protect it and the untold wealth it represents. Juggling that potential is a task of epic proportions and it's not long before a blonde angel and a trail of bodies assault Dak's belief structure and vault him into a chaotic twister of threats and mystery. The brutal murder of his best friend and his daughter's disappearance vaporize the lines between myth and reality. To save her and Juice, Dak faces a life-altering ultimatum in a pulse-pounding confrontation that will risk everything. Brace yourself for a thrill ride laced with humor, romance, secrets, and betrayals that unravel truths hidden since time began.

---

1. https://books2read.com/u/38J6OL

2. https://books2read.com/u/38J6OL

Read more at www.michaelpclutton.com.

Also by Michael Clutton

Hooked On Reel Fishing
How to Tackle Saltwater Fishing
Big Game Fishing

The Juice Chronicles
Bloodlines: The Juice Chronicles

Your Great Big Grab Bag of Useless Helpful Tidbits
Charity Giving Donation Revelation

Watch for more at www.michaelpclutton.com.

About the Author

Michael P. Clutton isn't your typical storyteller. Since he was young, he loved drawing cartoons and writing stories, which not only kept him busy but also helped him learn more words. This early passion for fiction laid the foundation for his unique voice—rich, imaginative, and brimming with wit.

Michael's sarcastic and unique perspective on life adds intrigue to his daily routine and captivates those around him. Known for his quick wit and self-deprecating humor, he can generate a giggle or a guffaw at the drop of a hat. His creative toolbox is well-stocked with both artwork and the written word, making him a versatile and dynamic creator.

Discover the captivating world of Michael P. Clutton, an author who combines humor, heart, and a deep passion for creativity in his stories and art.

Read more at www.michaelpclutton.com.